Sam

Many thanks for your help on the Crossroads Mission

T

Tina Hodges

May God continue to guide & open doors of favour before you.

Every blessing in Christ,

Tina Hodges (St John's, Park)

Tina Hodges
LoveF1rst
c/o The Beacon Church of St Paul and St Leonard
331 Arbourthorne Road
Sheffield
South Yorkshire
S2 2FH

Lovef1rsttina@googlemail.com
www.lovef1rst.com

ISBN: 978 0 9567270 2 2

Acknowledgments

Many thanks to Charlotte and Katherine Turner, my editors (who both majored in English at University), whose help and feedback has been both helpful and illuminating;

Many thanks to David Whisson, whose humour and humility are always a delight, and who consistently portrays my playful imagination beyond my expectations;

Grateful thanks to Jeff Haynie, whose Sword of the Spirit and other 'faith art' are truly inspirational;

Sincere thanks again to Laura Jane's graphic art skill, and the helpful flexibility and enthusiasm with which she has created the book cover (and whose ability to combine stay-at-home 'Mom' with her Graphic Art design business is amazing);

This book is dedicated to all reading this book who are dedicated to being an Overcomer, and to Taking Back What The Enemy Has Stolen.

Contents

Introduction 7

Chapter One: Who's Your Daddy? 9

Chapter Two: Persistent Prayer 17

Chapter Three: Spirit-Led Action 35

Chapter Four: Living From the Overflow 47

Chapter Five: Soul-Proofing 57

Chapter Six: Dying Well 71

Chapter Seven: Life in Fullness 83

Chapter Eight: Living from a Heavenly Place 107

Chapter Nine: Woven Together 123

Chapter Ten: Knowing Your Rights 133

Chapter Eleven: Going for Gold 149

More Information 159

Introduction

What a mess! A broken burned out couple, crushed by their failure in ministry and business, limped along. Surrounded by "successful" Christians, their ravaged lives reeked of desolation and disgrace. Their dream to plant churches as a family, to pioneer the kingdom, now a hollow vision. Despair and a performance-driven faith blinded them to the reality of God's redemptive love and aloneness overwhelmed them. Clinging to God by their fingertips and crying out to Him for help, they recognised their need for tools to live in a different way.

Meeting Tina and Jasper Hodges changed their lives. Tina came alongside this family in love, with God-given wisdom and passion to see them fulfil their God-given destiny. She gave herself, her resources, and eventually the Vicarage, to support them as they began to recover what the enemy had stolen.

Rarely will you meet someone whose passion and anointing match up. In this book, Tina outlines the keys to equip you to take hold of what is rightfully yours as a child of the King of Kings. It is my privilege to commend Tina Hodges to you. Her willingness to believe that our Heavenly Dad is bigger than any mess we might be in is changing my family's life.

In May 2011, Jasper and Tina invited my husband and I to come and work as self-financing family workers in inner city Sheffield. With the tools in this book, we are learning to do life and ministry in a different way. Not many in the body of Christ would have risked their reputations on us. This weekend we are baptising some of the first fruits of our ministry here in Arbourthorne & Norfolk Park. I am immensely grateful to God for bringing us Tina. This woman has revelation that could change your life and the lives of those around you.

If you want to know how to break free from sin, overcome the enemy and live the abundant life Jesus died to give you, this book is for you.

Sarah Halliwell
Family Worker

CHAPTER 1

Who's Your Daddy?

Daddy in the Detail

> *... the eyes of your understanding being enlightened; that you may know what is the hope of His calling, what are the riches of the glory of His inheritance in the saints, and what is the exceeding greatness of His power toward us who believe, according to the working of His mighty power which He worked in Christ when He raised Him from the dead and seated Him at His right hand in the heavenly places...* (Ephesians 1:18-20 NLT)

You might wonder what this topic has to do with Taking Back What's Been Stolen, but if we don't know Who We Are in the first place, how do we know our family or rights? God created us to be His. We're precious. We're dearly loved. We have immense value, but for those of us who don't yet know that on a deep level, it will very much affect our sense of self-worth and who we are, because if we don't realise that we are dearly loved children of Cod, then wc won't be aware of who we are or anything that we have to reclaim.

I went from the UK to a conference in America, and my husband, Jasper, encouraged me not to get any money beforehand, as the currency rate was more favourable if I got money there. However, I got off the plane, and the place where you usually get money exchanged was closed; ATMs – none of them accepted my card; my husband was 6 or 8 hours behind me on another plane, and I was in a city I'd not visited before, with no way to get to my hotel. So I prayed, and eventually, that led me to a woman who directed me to where some complementary shuttle coaches were taking passengers to hotels. My hotel was not as popular as the others, but after about an hour, my free courtesy hotel bus arrived and took me to the hotel. I kept my spirits up by praising God.

I arrived ravenous, put my stuff in my room, and was wondering how best to feed myself. I wandered down to the café, to see what the options were. It was about 8 o'clock in the evening, and the café wasn't open until the following day. I could have eaten a horse! While I was stood there, a woman in front of me was warming up some Thanksgiving dinner in a microwave, which smelt delicious. (Coincidentally, I had wanted to host a Thanksgiving dinner with our church staff team before I travelled, but hadn't had enough time. I was remembering this, as I smelt turkey and sweet potatoes warming.)

Suddenly, the woman turned round to me and asked 'Would you like to come for dinner?' I was shocked. I hadn't said anything; I was just looking up at the menu. After a moment's stunned silence, I said 'That's very kind,' and she explained that they'd got plenty to go around, and took me up to her room. She and her husband were very welcoming, and I discovered that her husband was a Pastor, and that they were from Memphis. Their grandson was travelling with them, and his name caught my attention, as he was called 'J-man', the same affectionate name that my daughters had given their step-father. I smiled at the fact that my hosts were both Pastors, like my husband and I, and that they, too, had a J-man in their family. As soon as I walked into the room, the gentleman said 'The Lord told us someone was coming for dinner!' I sat down, astonished both at the surprise meal and at the warmth of the company. I was blessed by how God had provided for me, before I'd even prayed about it, and when Jasper arrived, the couple insisted on driving to the airport to collect him. We had a lovely time with them, and Jasper ate like a king as well, before we retired for the night. We had much in common with them and they, too, had a big emphasis on youth and families in their small church.

When I was recounting this story to a couple of guys on our conference, they said straight away: 'Who's your Daddy?' in that charismatic and enthusiastic American way, indeed demonstrating His great love for me and the fact He was looking after the details in my life. Interesting that it was the guys that spotted it first!

Do You Know You're Invited?

You see, our 'filters' will determine whether or not we notice God's working quietly in our life. God is always there, watching, waiting, like the father waiting for the prodigal son to return. Sometimes, our own fears and rejections can hold us back; sometimes accusing thoughts can prevent us from even recognising the depth of intimacy that is ours for the taking; there isn't a problem on God's side, there's just often a blindness or ignorance on ours.

> *For God may speak in one way, or in another, yet man does not perceive it.* (Job 33:14 NKJV)

> *For as many as are led by the Spirit of God, these are sons of God. For you did not receive the spirit of bondage again to fear, but you received the Spirit of adoption by whom we cry out, "Abba, Father."* (Romans 8:14-15 NKJV)

If we don't know how much God loves and forgives us, we're not going to approach Him or walk closely with Him, and we're not going to say to Him *'Help!'* when we need Him. Not only that, but once we begin to grasp Who We Really Are In Christ, our destiny can then unfold, as we take hold of our inheritance as His sons and daughters, and begin to act like mini-Christs.

We begin to recognise that the enemy has no right to steal from us like he does, and that not only does God care about our situation, He cares enough to send Jesus as the solution, so that we can Take Back What The Enemy Has Stolen. Jesus restored the intimacy we were created to have with God, for which I am forever grateful.

However, we need to have a clear enough grasp of God as our loving Dad before we can begin to operate in our true authority. Once we know who our Daddy is (supreme God of the universe!) and what He wants for us, we have a clearer idea of Who We Are In Christ, and who we are lovingly created to be.

Trash Police

I know many people who have a low self esteem because they judge their worth by what has happened to them, and these thoughts and feelings then become rooted in how they think of themselves. *"You're no good! Call yourself a Christian? Hypocrite!"* This kind of 'thought trash' is not who we are.

It's just that we pick up spiritual 'nits' from such things, which need sorting before they discourage us. I've spent more than 40 years NOT realising that my thoughts didn't originate with me. I used to have many such thoughts of different kinds, aimed at myself and others, and I defined my worth by the Radio Crap playing in my head. How blind was I?

Imagine waking up one day and finding yourself in a sewer – where everyone's poo is sent. If you never have an idea of who you really are, you wake up stinking and think to yourself, what is happening? Everyone keeps throwing more crap at me. Either I am a piece of crap (a turd) or I am a toilet. If someone didn't come along and tell you otherwise, would you think yourself to be anything else? Doubtful.

This is what I imagine God would say to you: *"Actually, you're NOT a piece of crap. You're precious, and the crap that happened should never have happened to you, because you are SO precious. You may not believe it, but I, your heavenly Father, created you to be so much more! There are some crappy thought patterns which need to be broken by you realising Who You Are In Me, so that you can come and be fully connected with this place of purity and freedom where I dwell – THIS is Who I Created You To Be. Come out of the sewer and become who I created you to be. You could stay there and be who you think you are, or you could follow Me and let Me 'transform you by the renewal of your mind.' Make a decision to stop defining yourself by what happened to you – TODAY is the day of salvation. As soon as you can get your head round the fact that this smelly person with unwelcome thoughts is NOT the real you, then you and I can start your re-creation."*

> *We are more than conquerors through Him who loved us.*
> (Romans 8:37 NKJV)

Have Faith to Keep Going

As we come close to God, the process makes us see our sin before we see our Saviour. This is normal, but many people get stuck there. We need to keep travelling along the process, so that we see God's mercy recreating our hearts. Being sin-conscious is not yet the fullness of life Jesus spoke about; until His glory can outshine whatever mistakes we may have made, we are still in transit.

Our Daddy loves us – immeasurably!

You may be tempted to skip over this chapter thinking, *'I know all this already'* – but I would say, *'Really?'* You see, I can tell the extent to which God's love is deeply embedded in people by the way they act when disasters come their way. Does fear take over (as someone said to me recently *'bad things do happen to good people'*)? Do you fight, but then give up when things don't change?

I am often saddened that we lack revelation-knowledge (truth from the Holy Spirit which can free us). We generally need to see enough in order to believe.

In Isaiah 61 we see lots of restoration, but here are just a few things that we need to recognise as revelation-knowledge:

- The Spirit chooses to partner with us to bring good news to those who need it most. Poverty isn't just monetary – it can be everything. No friends. No hope. No joy. No one to trust. It can also partially be where we limit what we think God can do. Poverty mindsets suffocate what the gospel stands for. Fullness is what Jesus promised – not half-measures!

- We are sent to declare release to the captives – which, in my book, means declaring freedom over all who are imprisoned in their spirit, character, destiny, etc.

- Recovery of sight to the blind – revelation! Sight, where previously there has been blindness!

- To make free those who are oppressed – spiritually, relationally, etc.

- To declare the year of the Lord's favour – to make sure that when this happens, I take note that this is because Our Daddy Loves Us.

I challenge you as you read this book to ask the Holy Spirit to remind you of what areas the enemy has stolen from your life or those you love, and allow Him to stir your true identity, to help you rise up and take hold of your true authority – not just for your sake, but for the sake of the Kingdom.

Who's Your Daddy?

CHAPTER 2

Persistent Prayer

I look at a stone cutter hammering away at a rock a hundred times without so much as a crack showing in it. Yet at the 101st blow it splits in two. I know it was not the one blow that did it, but all that had gone before. (Anon)

Encouraged to Nag!

There's a passage in the Bible where Jesus tells a story about a persistent widow, a sort of nagging woman, really, who demands justice from a judge against her adversary. The judge decides to help, not because of any concern about what God thinks about his actions, nor out of any concern for the woman's wellbeing or right to justice, but because of the nagging woman wearing him out with her constant nagging – he just wants to get her out of his hair! Jesus, when telling this story, goes on to say *'how much more will God hear those who cry out to Him day and night?'*

> *One day Jesus told his disciples a story to show that they should always pray and never give up. "There was a judge in a certain city," he said, "who neither feared God nor cared about people. A widow of that city came to him repeatedly, saying, 'Give me justice in this dispute with my enemy.' The judge ignored her for a while, but finally he said to himself, 'I don't fear God or care about people, but this woman is driving me crazy.*

> *I'm going to see that she gets justice, because she is wearing me out with her constant requests!'''*
>
> *Then the Lord said, ''Learn a lesson from this unjust judge. Even he rendered a just decision in the end. So don't you think God will surely give justice to his chosen people who cry out to him day and night? Will he keep putting them off? I tell you, he will grant justice to them quickly! But when the Son of Man returns, how many will he find on the earth who have faith?''* (Luke 18:1-8a NLT)

There's something about persistence in prayer that oozes out of the Bible; there are lots of verses that talk about praying continually and praying without giving up.

This is all stuff that the Church is familiar with, but my observation is that very few people know how to really pray *without getting discouraged,* so they end up giving up.

Praying and not giving up requires us to keep ourselves encouraged while we're praying, to *know* that God hears us, to *know* that He will answer at the right time, but most of all, to know our Daddy *is* bigger than what we're facing and *He is sovereign.*

Persevering in Prayer

I want to share a story to illustrate what I'm talking about: after my daughters' Dad left our marriage after 20 years, both daughters were deeply affected, and it was very difficult for them for at least a couple of years. It wasn't until I re-married that my eldest daughter's issues surfaced, and she realised how much emotional hurt was still buried regarding her Dad leaving. As her painful issues surfaced and she struggled to know how to handle them, her boyfriend persuaded her to move to his town and live with him and his parents. This, combined with other pressures, caused her to leave home at 16. It all happened very suddenly from our point of view. I received a text message to say that she had gone. I was devastated. Not only had the enemy stolen my first husband (who had left to make a home with another married woman, who used to be a trusted friend), but the enemy had now taken my eldest daughter.

I had seen the enemy at work for the previous few months, but I didn't think that my daughter would just up and go. I felt heartbroken and, once again, robbed. I had a prophecy at the time, from Isabel Allum, and the first thing she said was

'The enemy's been stealing from you.'

I thought '*Too right, he has!*'

Lots of friends were telling me that Kitty, my eldest, was at the age where she should be allowed to do what she wants, and that the right thing to do was to just let her go. I didn't have a problem with letting her go at the right time, but I could see that the enemy was stealing from her, and us, in all that happened; I wasn't sure their advice was biblically-based or Spirit-led. I'd always anticipated that when she left home, she would be going off to university, and I had pictured me driving her there, car piled high with boxes – not have her leaving suddenly and dramatically like this.

For the best part of a week after she left, she never spoke to me at all; I didn't know what was happening and cried myself to sleep every night. I began to try and re-build our relationship, being as gentle and loving as I could, but I was quite devastated about what was going on. Most of my friends continued to tell me that I should let her go, but I had a very strong sense that because the enemy had been stealing, I shouldn't just sit back and let him continue to steal.

I asked Bill Johnson what I should do at a Question and Answer session on Healing at a New Wine Leaders Conference.

He said, *'She will always be your daughter and you will always have a spiritual authority over her, no matter what age she is. You bind the enemy, you loose the Kingdom. You battle when you can, you rest when you can't.'*

What he said felt so right in my spirit, so that's what I did. I took hold of my spiritual authority not just as a mother, but as a Child of God and a prayer warrior, and ignored the advice of others which was not God-led, albeit well-meaning.

Every time I prayed, every time I had a conversation with Kitty where I heard or saw the enemy influencing her (through blindness, lies etc.). I bound the enemy in prayer. I just loved her as best I could, but at the same time I was praying for God's Kingdom to be released. Where I saw blindness, I prayed for Kingdom revelation – I bound the blindness and loosed revelation. (Matthew 18:18)

When I had the energy, I prayed, and when I didn't, I just let God carry the situation. *I based my confidence to persevere not on what I could see, but on knowing I was using the right principles, so that I didn't get discouraged when things didn't look so good.*

That conference where I spoke to Bill Jonson was in the May. In that July, we visited Bill Johnson's church – Bethel Church – to attend their first ever Healing School, and both my daughters came along. On the first Sunday there, all the international visitors were invited to stand, which we did. Once we were standing, they said that they would like to bless us and asked us to walk to the front. The girls looked a little reluctant (!) but went up with us anyway. We stood in a row waiting to be prayed for, and there were about 30 members of staff to pray for about 150 people. When Bill Johnson came down from the stage, guess who was the first person he prayed for? Kitty. My firstborn! She was in tears, deeply affected by what was happening and I just KNEW, as soon as it was Bill who prayed for her, that God *had been* hearing my prayers. I didn't say anything to Bill about it, but when the service finished, a gentleman I had noticed earlier came up to us as we were heading for our car. He asked to pray for Kitty. We stood under the twigs of a tree in the blistering heat, and one of the first things he said to her was:

'Do you know Johnny Depp?' What he didn't know was that Johnny Depp was one of her favourite actors.

The gentleman then asked if she'd seen *Pirates of the Caribbean*, which happened to be a favourite movie of our daughters', and then went on to say:

'You know how Johnny Depp (Jack Sparrow) always wanted a boat of his own? Well, God is saying that He's your boat and that everything you're ever going to need is in Him.'

I melted when I heard this, as it was just what Kitty needed to hear. I asked her afterwards how she felt, and she said *'Special.'* That incident just really encouraged me to persevere in prayer, particularly in situations which appear hopeless.

When we came back from the States, Kitty started to properly consider her relationship with her boyfriend (without my input) and although it took a few months, by the January she had finished with him. All this time we were praying and being encouraged because we could see that we were able to Take Back What The Enemy Was Stealing through prayer. During those few months between returning from America and finishing with her boyfriend, she grew in revelation and understanding a bit at a time. As a parent, I learned to choose my battles; but if I saw things that I found difficult, I took it to God in prayer, blessing and loving our daughter first, whilst binding the enemy where he was at work and loosing the Kingdom.

When Kitty eventually 'came home', just after her exams at college in the May, I was able to help her pack up the car and take her off to university in the September, just like I'd always wanted. We all celebrated when she came home (almost killing the fatted calf!). It was a great day in more than one sense.

Since that time, mine and Kitty's relationship has deepened, and it's probably better than it's ever been. She is a gifted and compassionate girl who now believes in the power of persistent prayer as I do.

I believe, like Jesus said, that in prayer, we mustn't give up; but *we need to know about – and be convinced of – our authority, in order to be relentless.* The thing that I would say is, I prayed every day for Kitty. Sometimes several times a day, for over two years; always binding the enemy and releasing the Kingdom, battling when I could, and resting when I couldn't. I encourage you to persist in prayer. It works... Even when it feels like it doesn't.

Defeating Discouragement

One of the reasons that we fail to persist in prayer is because we become so discouraged that things won't change that we lose hope. So the must-win battle here is with our mind, will, and emotions; we need to fix them on the right things in order to stay encouraged. In the Bible, we are told to do this in several places. Here are just a few:

> *If then you were raised with Christ, seek those things which are above, where Christ is, sitting at the right hand of God. Set your mind on things above, not on things on the earth. For you died, and your life is hidden with Christ in God.* (Colossians 3:1-3 NKJV)

For God has not given us a spirit of fear, but of power and of love and of a sound mind. (2 Timothy 1:7 NKJV)

Not that I have already attained, or am already perfected; but I press on, that I may lay hold of that for which Christ Jesus has also laid hold of me. Brethren, I do not count myself to have apprehended; but one thing I do, forgetting those things which are behind and reaching forward to those things which are ahead, I press toward the goal for the prize of the upward call of God in Christ Jesus. (Philippians 3:12-14 NKJV)

We can lose hope when we allow recurring problems to gradually become bigger in our perspective until they seem bigger than God, all because of repetition. Don't let the enemy fool you – your past does not have to dictate your future. All the time you think it will, it will!

One of my favourite stories of inspiring perseverance is that of Thomas Edison. He was labelled "stupid" and "unteachable" by teachers and was eventually removed from school altogether by his parents when he was still a young boy. His teenage years consisted of working various jobs and being fired from them all. Yet this incredible individual never stopped inventing, acquiring a total of 1,093 patents throughout his life. The majority of his work failed, but the successful minority were revolutionary: the lightbulb, the stock printer, the phonograph and the alkaline battery. It is Edison that can be credited for defining genius as "1% inspiration and 99% perspiration".

One particular part of his life that is especially inspiring happened after he had already become successful with the invention of the lightbulb. Because the ore that was used for lightbulb filaments had high shipping costs (it was mined in the

Midwest at the time), Edison made it his mission to run an ore mining plant in New Jersey. Despite committing almost a decade to the plant, and acquiring 47 patents for inventions within it to help it run more efficiently, the plant failed due to the poor quality of East Coast ore. But one of those 47 inventions eventually became groundbreaking in the cement industry and earned Edison back almost all the money he had lost in his failed enterprise. Henry Ford later credited Edison's project as the chief inspiration behind his legendary Model T Ford assembly line.

Edison's commitment and dedication to the ore-mining plant resulted in huge success, despite initial signs of failure.

Focussing Rightly

We can also lose hope by becoming worn out by hanging on in there, so how we focus our gaze, spiritually, will really determine whether or not we can persist and keep our hope up. Do your eyes focus on the problem, or is God bigger? Can you take your concerns and turn them to God, for what He plans to do? I say this because I made a fundamental transition the day I did.

I used to get frustrated about a recurrent issue over someone's behaviour which affected me, but whilst I was still feeling affected by it, I realised the enemy was using my reaction to get a foothold. So I changed my approach, in order to prevent it getting me down.

I started acknowledging that God was bigger than this issue; that He had already heard my prayer and was acting on it, and I said *'I can't WAIT to see how you're going to make this one work out'*. That has become a mantra for me now – whenever I'm beginning to feel overwhelmed, I just take my thoughts and feelings and set them on God and say *'I can't wait to see how you're going to handle this,'* and He always does. At first I said it by faith, as I didn't truly feel it. Now I feel it and am excited (I know that sounds strange!) when I say it, as I'm truly standing back to give God an opportunity to demonstrate His glory. My whole mindset has become renewed.

> *Therefore we also, since we are surrounded by so great a cloud of witnesses, let us lay aside every weight, and the sin which so easily ensnares us, and let us run with endurance the race that is set before us, looking unto Jesus, the author and finisher of our faith, who for the joy that was set before Him endured the cross, despising the shame, and has sat down at the right hand of the throne of God.* (Hebrews 12:1-2 NKJV)
>
> Marinating ourselves in what God has said is not new.
>
> *He took me there, and behold, there was a man whose appearance was like the appearance of bronze. He had a line of flax and a measuring rod in his hand, and he stood in the gateway.*
>
> *And the man said to me, "Son of man, look with your eyes and hear with your ears, and fix your mind on everything I show you; for you were brought here so that I might show them to you. Declare to the house of Israel everything you see."* (Ezekiel 40:3-4 NKJV)

Ezekiel was asked by his heavenly visitor to fix his mind (and his heart) on what he was being shown. We can look and see, we can listen and hear, but to really take things on board, we need to fix our mind and heart on what God shows us.

Defeating Distractions

The other thing that can wear us out and take us off track is distractions. That's one of the tactics the enemy uses to bring us discouragement and he knows what distracts each and every one of us. He'll have us running after our tail over unimportant things which will wear us out so that we don't have the energy for the important things. Recognising this tactic of his, and learning to prioritise the important things, helps beat this.

Our church recently opened a cafe and we realised that someone was stealing from the till. We decided to implement a checking process which would quietly prevent the person from stealing. So, by implementing the process, we sorted the initial problem, which meant that we weren't pressured by time constraints in dealing with the person at the time. The enemy isn't likely to change his tactics of distraction, but we can set processes in place which help us overcome.

I have a number of processes that help keep distractions at bay. Let me share them with you:

- Remember that God heard you the first time you prayed and will answer at the very best time for you. He knows all, therefore He knows best when the time to answer is optimum.

- Remind Him of your request regularly and of your confidence in His answer. It keeps the anticipation of His answer fresh in your mind, as well as expressing your confidence in His goodness.

- Restrain live emotion – live emotion is not driven by the Holy Spirit. In fact, it prevents us from hearing the Spirit clearly, so do not allow yourself to become overwhelmed with discouraging feelings. Take them to the cross.

Feelings rarely tell anyone the truth or lead us towards God, unless they are whole and sanctified. I choose not to make major decisions in live emotion because of this.

- Rest and recuperate – there's not a lot that a good night's sleep, a good meal and love from friends can't strengthen – these are part of my self-encouragement strategy.

- Recognise that perspective is rarely 100% objective truth, though subjective truth has its place. It may help us to recognise how to care for ourselves better and what may be stopping us from being open in our spirit to greater revelation.

Have you not known?
Have you not heard?
The everlasting God, the LORD,
The Creator of the ends of the earth,
Neither faints nor is weary.
His understanding is unsearchable.
He gives power to the weak,
And to those who have no might He increases strength.
Even the youths shall faint and be weary,
And the young men shall utterly fall,
But those who wait on the LORD
Shall renew their strength;
They shall mount up with wings like eagles,
They shall run and not be weary,
They shall walk and not faint. (Isaiah 40:28-31 NKJV)

Our perspective is shaped by so many things: how encouraged we feel, how rested and fresh we are, and how secure and strengthened in our spirit we are. All these things become renewed as we wait on God. I encourage people to learn 'cherishing strategies', so they can overcome challenges in life. It is important that we all learn how to keep our own spirit cherished; in other words, how to strengthen ourselves in the Lord (Bill Johnson wrote an excellent book called Strengthen Yourself In The Lord which I wholeheartedly recommend!). Also, my cherishing book *'Learning To Love Yourself'*.

Praise-Shaped Perspective as a Weapon

Strengthening yourself includes ensuring that that you're prioritising quality time with God, making time to have real fun, and prioritising those things that you're passionate about, thus not allowing yourself to get into discouragement. I remember hearing Bill Johnson say once that when he feels discouraged, he shuts himself away to spend time with God (in worship) until he is feeling better. I was so encouraged to hear that, because I do the same. Worship is the very first thing I turn to when I am discouraged. It brings a necessary alignment in my spirit that I need if I am going to function like a child of God in my thoughts and actions.

In 2 Chronicles 20, we read how Israel's enemy was thrown into confusion when God's people began to praise Him for who He was and what He had done in the past. Talk about rubbing the enemy's nose in it! I've included the whole story because it has many nuggets in it.

> *It happened after this that the people of Moab with the people of Ammon, and others with them besides the Ammonites, came to battle against Jehoshaphat. Then some came and told Jehoshaphat, saying, "A great multitude is coming against you from beyond the sea, from Syria; and they are in Hazazon Tamar" (which is En Gedi). And Jehoshaphat feared, and set*

himself to seek the LORD, and proclaimed a fast throughout all Judah. So Judah gathered together to ask help from the LORD; and from all the cities of Judah they came to seek the LORD.

Then Jehoshaphat stood in the assembly of Judah and Jerusalem, in the house of the LORD, before the new court, and said: "O LORD God of our fathers, are You not God in heaven, and do You not rule over all the kingdoms of the nations, and in Your hand is there not power and might, so that no one is able to withstand You? Are You not our God, who drove out the inhabitants of this land before Your people Israel, and gave it to the descendants of Abraham Your friend forever? And they dwell in it, and have built You a sanctuary in it for Your name, saying, 'If disaster comes upon us – sword, judgment, pestilence, or famine – we will stand before this temple and in Your presence (for Your name is in this temple), and cry out to You in our affliction, and You will hear and save.' And now, here are the people of Ammon, Moab, and Mount Seir – whom You would not let Israel invade when they came out of the land of Egypt, but they turned from them and did not destroy them – here they are, rewarding us by coming to throw us out of Your possession which You have given us to inherit. O our God, will You not judge them? For we have no power against this great multitude that is coming against us; nor do we know what to do, but our eyes are upon You."

Now all Judah, with their little ones, their wives, and their children, stood before the LORD.

Then the Spirit of the LORD came upon Jahaziel the son of Zechariah, the son of Benaiah, the son of Jeiel, the son of Mattaniah, a Levite of the sons of Asaph, in the midst of the assembly. And he said, "Listen, all you of Judah and you inhabitants of Jerusalem, and you, King Jehoshaphat! Thus says the LORD to you: 'Do not be afraid nor dismayed because of this great multitude, for the battle is not yours, but God's. Tomorrow go down against them. They will surely come up by the Ascent of Ziz, and you will find them at the end of the brook before the Wilderness of Jeruel. You will not need to fight in this battle. Position yourselves, stand still and see the salvation of the LORD, who is with you, O Judah and Jerusalem!' Do not fear or be dismayed; tomorrow go out against them, for the LORD is with you."

And Jehoshaphat bowed his head with his face to the ground, and all Judah and the inhabitants of Jerusalem bowed before the LORD, worshiping the LORD. Then the Levites of the children of the Kohathites and of the children of the Korahites stood up to praise the LORD God of Israel with voices loud and high.

So they rose early in the morning and went out into the Wilderness of Tekoa; and as they went out, Jehoshaphat stood and said, "Hear me, O Judah and you inhabitants of Jerusalem: Believe in the LORD your God, and you shall be established; believe His prophets, and you shall prosper." And when he had consulted with the people, he appointed those who should sing to the LORD, and who should praise the beauty of holiness, as they went out before the army and were saying:

"Praise the LORD, for His mercy endures forever."

Now when they began to sing and to praise, the LORD set ambushes against the people of Ammon, Moab, and Mount Seir, who had come against Judah; and they were defeated. For the people of Ammon and Moab stood up against the inhabitants of Mount Seir to utterly kill and destroy them. And when they had made an end of the inhabitants of Seir, they helped to destroy one another.

So when Judah came to a place overlooking the wilderness, they looked toward the multitude; and there were their dead bodies, fallen on the earth. No one had escaped.

When Jehoshaphat and his people came to take away their spoil, they found among them an abundance of valuables on the dead bodies, and precious jewellery, which they stripped off for themselves, more than they could carry away; and they were three days gathering the spoil because there was so much. And on the fourth day they assembled in the Valley of Berachah, for there they blessed the LORD; therefore the name of that place was called The Valley of Berachah until this day. Then they returned, every man of Judah and Jerusalem, with Jehoshaphat in front of them, to go back to Jerusalem with joy, for the LORD had made them rejoice over their enemies. So they came to Jerusalem, with stringed instruments and harps and trumpets, to the house of the LORD. And the fear of God was on all the kingdoms of those countries when they heard that the LORD had fought against the enemies of Israel. Then the realm of Jehoshaphat was quiet, for his God gave him rest all around. (2 Chronicles 20:1-30 NKJV)

Note that praise glorifies God and keeps our focus on His nature and power. It throws the enemy into confusion and causes our spirit to become encouraged before we even see God's favour manifested.

Everyone has a time when they feel the enemy, or their problem, is bigger than God. Jehoshaphat was king, and even he didn't know what to do about Israel's old enemies turning up and banding together – talk about pressure! So those of us who are leaders are in good company. We need to keep our perspective uncluttered by fear if we're going to be in this for the long haul. My husband Jasper, when he's going through a difficult time, sometimes closes his eyes and imagines a large angel next to him, a small problem in front of him, and a giant vision of Jesus behind and above the problem. The enemy always steals from us when our perspective is shaped by unhealthy fear and not love.

> *There is no fear in love; but perfect love casts out fear, because fear involves torment. But he who fears has not been made perfect in love.* (1 John 4:18 NKJV)

Worship will always attract the Holy Spirit (John 4:23-24) and the Holy Spirit will always lead us into all truth (John 16:13), especially truth that shapes our perspective rightly so we can hear God, step up, and take back!

Ensuring Your Action is Blessed

It is worth noting, as I end this chapter, that Jehosophat had learnt to enquire of the Lord. Remember to enquire of God over decisions, and not assume you have heard God's direction before He shows you. There are many of us, I suspect, who start something in the Spirit and later stray into our own way of doing things. We cannot expect that persevering in prayer will be blessed just because of our perseverance – we need to ensure, at all times, that we have heard from the Lord, if we are expecting His blessing.

David, in 1 Samuel 23, was used to enquiring of the Lord; when his followers lost heart because of fear, he double-checked that he had heard the Lord rightly. He had, and he was able to help quell his men's fear by reassuring them of his enquiry and the consequent answer. They went on to Take Back What The Enemy Was Stealing.

> *Then they told David, saying, "Look, the Philistines are fighting against Keilah, and they are robbing the threshing floors."*
>
> *Therefore David inquired of the LORD, saying, "Shall I go and attack these Philistines?"*
>
> *And the LORD said to David, "Go and attack the Philistines, and save Keilah."*
>
> *But David's men said to him, "Look, we are afraid here in Judah. How much more then if we go to Keilah against the armies of the Philistines?" Then David inquired of the LORD once again.*
>
> *And the LORD answered him and said, "Arise, go down to Keilah. For I will deliver the Philistines into your hand." And David and his men went to Keilah and fought with the Philistines, struck them with a mighty blow, and took away their livestock. So David saved the inhabitants of Keilah.* (1 Samuel 23:1-5 NKJV)

When enquiring of the Lord myself, I aim not to have any desires or expectations of my own in my mind and heart – not a particular answer that I would like God to say. To do otherwise would be to prejudice my discernment.

"Son of man, these leaders have set up idols in their hearts. They have embraced things that will make them fall into sin. Why should I listen to their requests? Tell them, 'This is what the Sovereign LORD says: The people of Israel have set up idols in their hearts and fallen into sin, and then they go to a prophet asking for a message. So I, the LORD, will give them the kind of answer their great idolatry deserves.'" (Ezekiel 14:3-4 NLT)

I have learnt to 'die' to what I want before asking God anything (I expand on this in another chapter). Where I recognise I still need to die, or, like David, need reassurance that I've heard rightly, I will ask others to discern on my behalf, something I am sure will continue to be a major part of my life this side of heaven.

The man who mobilises the Christian church to pray will make the greatest contribution to world evangelisation in history. (Andrew Murray)

Persistent Prayer

CHAPTER 3

Spirit-Led Action

For all who are led by the Spirit of God are children of God. (Romans 8:14 NLT)

James the Apostle said *'Faith without works is dead.'* Discerning the right action as the Spirit leads us is key to *Taking Back What The Enemy Has Stolen.* Whenever we follow the Holy Spirit's leading, even though we may not be aware of it, we are pushing back the enemy's territory. We are ushering in God's Kingdom, which is a Kingdom of light, and the enemy's domain, the darkness, is pushed back. I love all the stories in the book of Acts which demonstrate this particular principle.

The Spirit Leading Me to Sheffield

When God called me to Sheffield, I had been on a conference the week before at St. Thomas Crookes and it was my first visit into Sheffield centre. I was deeply impressed with The Order of Mission, and thought to myself, as I returned to the town where I was Team Vicar, that I would join The Order of Mission when I got home. It was something I could join anywhere which would link me to like-minded people. I arrived home on the Saturday, and on the Monday I had a call from a prophetic intercessor friend from Kent, saying:

'I think God's calling you to Sheffield.'

And I said *'Really? Well He's not told me! If God's calling me to Sheffield I want to hear 'Sheffield' from two other people.'*

On the Wednesday, I had a call from another prophetic intercessor friend from The Isle of Man. The two friends didn't know each other, and she also said:

'I think God's calling you to Sheffield.'

I thought *'Ok God, you've got my interest now.'* I logged it mentally, and just kept open about it. On the Friday, I was doing some outreach to night-clubbers at two o'clock in the morning, and this guy just walks up to me and shouts:

'Sheffield!' in his strange, drunken drawl.

'What?' I said, a bit stunned.

'Sheffield', he reiterated.

I asked what he meant and he said:

'You're from Sheffield aren't you?'

I thought, *'Do I sound like I'm from Sheffield?* (I thought I had quite a posh, Southern accent.)

And then I remembered: I had said to God that I wanted to 'hear *'Sheffield'* from two other people.'

God had done that. So the next morning, I emailed my Bishop and mentioned the incident to him and asked him to pray.

I arranged a visit to see my Bishop, and when Bishop Colin and I were talking he said that it sounded *'Interesting.'* He encouraged me to discern whether or not it was God calling me to Sheffield. I was 3 years into an 8 year contract in a Team Ministry, my marriage had broken down the year before, and despite being unsure about things that were happening with me personally, I had no intention of moving.

I wrote to the leaders at St. Thomas' Crookes and Philadelphia, as they were the only churches I knew in Sheffield (from the conference I attended a week or two before). I said that I thought God might be calling me to Sheffield. They politely said *'We don't think so!'* I'm guessing I wasn't the first to say this after attending their Pilgrimage. I really wasn't itching to move to Sheffield, as the last thing I wanted to do was uproot my girls, as they'd only just started to settle down after their

Dad had left. I really didn't have a clue what to do.

I went to see a priest friend, Viv, and she asked what was new. I said that I might be moving to Sheffield. I told her the story of the three words about Sheffield.

She asked *'Where to?'*

'I have no idea', I said.

She said *'You could stay in my flat.'*

I had no idea that she had any connection with Sheffield, as she lived near Leamington, but she went on to explain that her daughter had been to university in Sheffield, and had lived in the flat that they had bought.

'It became available yesterday,' she said, handing me the keys, *'Go and have a look at it.'*

So, later in the week, my youngest daughter and I drove up to have a look at the flat. It was perfect for us.

There were so many coincidences surrounding our move to Sheffield. For instance, my Aunt, who lives on the outskirts of Sheffield, asked where my youngest daughter would go to school if we moved. I honestly had no idea because I didn't know which part we were being called to. I just kept seeing a picture of our family teddy bear in my mind when I prayed about it, which was a bit weird, so I dismissed it. My Aunt kept going on about this great school that was in her area, but I knew God wouldn't be calling me to a more affluent area like hers. However, one day she let slip what the name of the school was; the school had the same name as our family teddy bear: *Ecgbert!* (The school was called King Ecgbert's) so I agreed to go and see it with my youngest daughter, and we were shown around. At the beginning of the tour, we were told that they had no places left, but by the end they offered her a place, there and then, and they had the very GCSE options that she wanted. Everything seemed to be perfectly planned ahead of our going there.

The weekend I visited my Aunt to talk about schools, I had thought that it would be a good idea to get in contact with the Bishop of Sheffield, just to introduce myself. The next morning, my Aunt invited me to a garden party for the Mother's Union, which just so happened to be at the Bishop's House. Guess who were the first two people I saw when I arrived? The Bishop of Sheffield and his assistant Bishop. As you can see, God made sure everything was in place.

When it came to making the decision about actually moving though, I was driving up to Sheffield to talk with Toby and Dave from St. Thomas', when I noticed, in the lay-by, a beige Mini. Now, this Mini was identical to one I had years ago, and it reminded me of a time in my life when, as a newly married couple, my first husband and I were quite poor. For the best part of a year, we didn't have a car, and couldn't afford to fix our old one. He was cycling to work and I was driving a Moped, and as I was doing up to 80 hours a week in shifts, matron-ing in a nursing home, it was a really hard time for us. So when I saw this beige Mini in the lay-by, I sensed that God was calling me to live by faith when I moved to Sheffield. But there was a real reluctance in my heart to live by faith. Everyone I knew at the time who lived by faith was poor and they all hinted about how poor they were, so it didn't appeal to me because poverty is nothing glorious and I didn't want to live by scrounging. I was very poor growing up and didn't want to return to it. It is true that the enemy increases his grip in poverty, not loosens it; I have to say, those I knew who lived by faith back then had a poverty complex and were not living dependent on God as true sons. So I was having a little internal battle after seeing this Mini in the lay-by, when all of a sudden my radio turned itself on. An old song came on:

All power is given in Jesus' name,
In Earth and Heaven in Jesus' name,
In Jesus' name I come to you
To share His power as He told me to.
Freely, freely you have received,
Freely, freely give.
Go in my name, and because you believe,
Others will know that I live.

My radio had just come on supernaturally, and it was the middle of Roger Royal's Sunday evening programme (that I didn't even know existed!). But as it happened, at the exact moment that I was having those fearful thoughts, I knew that God was trying to tell me something. So, I gave my fear to God about being poor and I said *'Have your way. I trust you.'* I knew God better than I used to and my trust had grown.

When I arrived for my meeting in Sheffield with Toby and Dave, I explained to them that I felt called to Sheffield, but didn't know what I was being called to do. At the end of our session, they prayed to God that if it was right for me to move to Sheffield, *'That you would show her open doors'*. Straight afterwards, I went to visit Jasper, who at the time was a new friend that I had met at the conference. When he prayed with me as I left, he said *'I don't usually get pictures, but I can see a picture of an open door, with the word 'Go' written on it'.*

Clear or what?

Can you see all the different confirmations? Can you see how God led me by His Spirit? Always when God leads me, He has me grow in understanding or confidence. His purposes for me are to find intimacy with Him – and to be the head and not the tail.

Much of the time in the Christian life, we don't wait for the Holy Spirit to lead us, we do things in whatever way we feel is right, because we are led by our mind or our urges which come from our feelings. Yet Jesus said that He did whatever He saw the Father do. How many of us can say that we're that Spirit-led about our day?

How many of us can say that when we get out of bed, we ask the Spirit what to do with our day, ask to be guided to the right people, ask to be shown what to pray for and how to pray for it? You may think that God only does this in special circumstances, but I don't believe that is true.

I recently did a 40 day fast, and towards the end of it, I had a bad throat virus and felt poorly. I was determined, however, if it was right, to finish the fast, and was praying about everything I was drinking. In the last week of the fast, Jasper and I were driving back from a meeting in London, and as we arrived at the service station, I saw a cafe latte in my mind as I prayed. Certain that it was a distraction from the enemy (and too close to my usual drink of choice), I dismissed it. It kept coming back. I shared my picture with Jasper, who agreed with my conclusion, but it kept coming back when I prayed. In the end, I realised that misled obedience was better than none, so I ordered the latte and within 5 minutes of drinking it, I was beginning to feel miraculously better. Knowing certain vitamins are lost when we drink coffee, I was at a loss to explain why I felt so good, so I 'googled' coffee and discovered it helped poor breathing and inflammation, which stunned me a little. Even the tiniest details of our lives are important to God, if only we are prepared to pay the price of learning to refer to the Holy Spirit in everything. I repented, knowing that my heavenly Daddy loves me and knows what is best for me.

The Spirit Transcends Our Rationale

The thing about Spirit-led action, which is important to grasp, is that we will NOT understand it with our mind, initially.

For those who are more thinking-led, like me, that can be an issue. But we need to recognise that our rationale is very limited compared to the mind of God, and God will work in such a way that we will not be able to see more than one step ahead of us. We're not meant to see the whole picture (our mind couldn't even conceive it even if we did, and it wouldn't feed our faith).

Sometimes, the situation we (or others) are facing is a challenging situation and we long to find a way through, to see a solution. God can show us a solution, but it usually starts with doing something that we don't understand with our rational minds. We need to believe in our heart that God sees the big picture and is leading us, like with the coffee story.

When I left the town I used to live in for Sheffield, rationally, people didn't understand. They thought I was running away, and they thought it was inappropriate to take my girls after they had lost their father, to give up the house and the income that we had in order to follow the Spirit's leading. Some church leaders even thought I was a little odd in following the Holy Spirit, but actually, God's strategy, and my following it obediently, meant that I got my fullness and my freedom a lot quicker. It meant that things changed for me really quickly. I found myself in favoured situations, all because I'd done as God had said.

Just because your rational mind doesn't understand it, doesn't mean that it's not God. Generally, you need to check to see whether or not what God is asking you to do agrees with the Bible, or whether or not there's a pattern and seek wisdom from friends, like my Bishop who said that my situation was interesting and worth pursuing. He knew I was called to Sheffield, and he too had no idea why, but his encouragement and wisdom helped me make my decision. It was only later that

I understood why I was called to Sheffield, and it wasn't just to fulfil ministry stuff; the move also led me to Jasper, my second husband. God has done a lot of restoration since I have moved to Sheffield, Taking Back What The Enemy Had Stolen from me, and my year of Jubilee started the summer I left for Sheffield.

> *Put very simply, Satan's power in the world is everywhere. Yet whenever men and women walk in the Spirit, sensitive to the anointing they have from God, that power of his just evaporates. There is a line drawn by God, a boundary whereby virtue of His own very presence Satan's writ does not run. Let God but occupy all the space Himself, and what room is left for the evil one?* (Watchman Nee)

How We Live by Faith

Seeing what is ahead is not living by faith, it's living by sight. If we're living by faith, and we're called to act a certain way by the Holy Spirit, then it'll only be the next step we must take that we are shown – we won't see the whole picture, and part of that is because God's picture is so much bigger than ours and we can't get our heads round it. Look at all the stories in Acts of the Apostles! Doesn't God's planning just blow your mind?

God makes us live by faith by showing us just what we need to see in order to make the next step, but He does not show us more until we are living by faith to such a degree that, like Moses, we see Him face to face and He shares His heart with us.

> *Oh, how great are God's riches and wisdom and knowledge! How impossible it is for us to understand his decisions and his ways! For who can know the Lord's thoughts? Who knows enough to give him advice?* (Romans 11:33-34 NLT)

We're not going to rely on God in the same way if we are fully relying on our senses and our ability to rationalise. Believing involves putting our WHOLE weight and trust in who God is and what He has said to us – which is a faith venture, not a sighted one!

> *He who believes in Me (who cleaves to and trusts in and relies on Me) as the Scripture has said, From his innermost being shall flow (continuously) springs and rivers of living water. But He was speaking here of the Spirit...* (John 7:38-39a Amplified)

Whilst we're not going to see the whole picture, if we see just the one step ahead, God will have the next step when we are ready for it. This tends to happen once our whole weight has been transferred onto that first step. Sometimes verbally committing ourselves to something is enough – but more often than not, our faith requires an act that demonstrates we truly are placing our trust in God.

But God doesn't call us to be comfortable. He calls us to trust Him so completely that we are afraid to put ourselves in situations where we will be in trouble if He doesn't come through. (Francis Chan: *Crazy Love: Overwhelmed By A Relentless God*)

When a climber climbs a cliff, he doesn't see all of the hand holds between the bottom and the top of the cliff ahead of time – he'll only see them one at a time as he comes to them. Once the climber has taken one step and moved, he can discern the next. That's what it's like living by faith; we see that one step and act on it, totally reliant on God. I've got hundreds of stories I could tell you about this, but they're all the same; they all exemplify 'one step at a time' and a whole-hearted commitment to step out without seeing more than one step ahead.

Keeping in Step with the Spirit

Much of what we do which is good is in vain, as it is not Spirit-led. I'd go so far to say that where we're not Spirit-led, we are outside of God's will. I say that humbly, knowing I've lived much of my life outside of God's will, but I don't want to waste any more time and don't wish that for you either. We can either live a good life, or God's life for us – I know which I'd prefer.

> *Remain in me, and I will remain in you. For a branch cannot produce fruit if it is severed from the vine, and you cannot be fruitful unless you remain in me. Yes, I am the vine; you are the branches. Those who remain in me, and I in them, will produce much fruit. For apart from me you can do nothing.* (John 15:4-5 NLT)

> *Now the things done may not be evil or improper; they in fact may be good and godly (such as reading the Bible, praying, worshiping, preaching); but if they are not undertaken in a spirit of complete reliance upon the Holy Spirit, then the flesh is the source of all. The old creation is willing to do anything – even to submit to God – if only it is permitted to live and to be active! (Watchman Nee)*

Many people fear giving their all to God, but that is madness! There is no one who has our interests, and the interests of those we love, more deeply rooted in His heart than God.

One of the things that I have prayed about for years is never wanting to be outside of God's will. I want to be slap-bang right in the middle of it. The times I've often found myself outside of God's will, I've either been too busy, too distracted, pressured, got the wrong end of the stick about something, or I've not heard something right. Usually character stuff and a lack of self-discipline has been my downfall, much as I would have liked to believe the issue was at God's end!

God will give us confirmation when we're truly seeking to be in His will, and I encourage you: follow biblical guidelines and if you're seeking God for guidance, then listen to Him and do what He says, through Scripture and the Spirit, whatever the cost. Additionally, seek out more mature Spirit-led Christian people who you trust to provide Spiritual Accountability, especially with the more important decisions.

> *And you will seek Me and find Me, when you search for Me with all your heart. I will be found by you, says the Lord, and I will bring you back from your captivity;* (Jeremiah 29:13-14a NKJV)

What if You Make a Mistake?

I have a recent example to put your heart at rest. Jasper and I were on a conference yesterday, deep in discussion about *'What if you are trying to follow God's will, yet getting it wrong?'*

I said to him, *'God will find a way of showing you'*. He loves us that much, that if we're truly seeking Him, yet are a bit off track, He will give us lots of signs to try and guide us.

At which point, we both looked up and noticed we were sitting in the wrong seminar! We apologised and found the right one, but I smiled at God confirming what I had just said by giving us an example.

See if there are patterns in your life that He's showing you, either through people that you know, or situations that are unusual; you will know when it's God speaking. It will cause you to pause and take note.

But it's important, as the Bible says, to test the spirits. In other words, use discernment when it comes to deciding whether it's the Holy Spirit you're following, or whether it's one of the enemy's distractions.

(If you find it hard to hear the Holy Spirit, there are a number of books and courses around that can assist with this. One book I would recommend is Mark Virkler's book *'4 Keys to Hearing God's Voice'.* (www.cwgministries.org/Four-Keys-to-Hearing-Gods-Voice). The Christian Leadership University which he is associated with also offers a range of courses to help you become more Spirit-led in different areas of life and ministry.)

If we're being Spirit-led, we'll be carrying a level of anointing that we'll be unaware of, because we're right in the middle of His will. There have been many times when I have had the confidence to speak up about something and it became clear that I was being Spirit-led; I could go up to someone I didn't know and share what God had put on my heart. If I wasn't being Spirit-led, I wouldn't necessarily feel compelled to do it. Where we're Spirit-led, we're automatically in the Lord's will.

Spirit-Led Action

CHAPTER 4

Living from the Overflow

Leaking His Presence

If you fill a glass with water all the way to the top, you've got enough to drink. But if you keep pouring water into the glass, then there would be an overflow. One of the things I've learnt in life is that where spiritual fruit naturally flows, where I've seen anointing and peace, where healing is present, is when there is an *overflow.*

In other words, out of an intimacy with God through marinating in His word, soaking in His presence, being submerged in His teaching, or just dwelling on different revelations, we then leak a power and presence which can only be described as an Overflow of God. When I'm in that place, that Overflow, I'm connected to an intimate, divine place, which is right in the Father's presence.

> *May the God of your hope so fill you with all joy and peace in believing (through the experience of your faith)* ***that by the power of the Holy Spirit you may abound and be overflowing*** *(bubbling over) with hope.* (Romans 15:13 Amplified)

There are two things that I want to talk about: one is about living from the Overflow, and the other, which is related to this, is being anchored and rooted in God.

Living From The Overflow

When we live from the Overflow, rather than just what's in the glass, we're living from a place of fullness and completeness in God, rather than living out of our own incompleteness. If we've not had life modelled well for us well as children, then it's very easy to live for other people's agendas, to put other people's priorities before God's perfect will for our lives.

Jesus made it clear that we were to love others as we love ourselves (in the same manner) and there is an assumption in His command that we love ourselves well – otherwise Jesus is saying we should hate others as we hate ourselves, which is definitely *not* what he meant.

I regularly spend time with people who are diagnosed with terminal illnesses, and in almost every case, they have grown up with habits of 'oughts' which have led them to live life for other people's expectations, rather than God's. Their lack of ability to self-love and care is spiritually and emotionally clear.

Life then becomes burdensome for them, and they begin to resent others who seemingly 'pressure them' because of their own absent self-care processes. To operate more healthily, we need to change looking out for others before looking out for ourselves – otherwise we are breaking the second commandment towards ourselves, as well as giving the enemy a sturdy foothold into our lives!

God never wants us not to love ourselves – He wants us to love ourselves very well and love others *as generously as we love ourselves.* I'm not talking about self-indulgence here, but self-care.

The two most important commandments are to love God first and then to love others as ourselves. There is a good reason it is this way round. Loving God first connects us intimately with our creator, heavenly Dad and God, who is the source of all love. Being connected to Him puts us in good stead for the next commandment.

"Teacher, which is the great commandment in the law?"

Jesus said to him, "'You shall love the Lord your God with all your heart, with all your soul, and with all your mind.' This is the first and great commandment.

And the second is like it: 'You shall love your neighbour as yourself.' On these two commandments hang all the Law and the Prophets." (Matthew 22:36-40 NKJV)

It's really important we don't skip over this without getting it. We love others out of knowing that we ourselves are loved and cherished by God, protected as we follow His loving ways for our lives. We love God, ourselves and others out of the Overflow of being loved by God.

We love (Him) because He first loved us.
(1 John 4:19 NKJV)

However, the reality is, many of us are still journeying in our relationship with God. It's like we are still half-orphan and half-son and may have picked up all sorts of bad habits, either because cherishing ourselves was not modelled well for us, or circumstances affected us. (Let me be clear: we are welcomed as 'sons' from the day we accept Jesus, but where there is a delay in taking off our old person and putting on the new person, the enemy makes the most of it!)

I breast fed my eldest daughter until she was 14 months, but my second daughter for just four months because I had a car accident which interrupted the intimacy I had with her. Years later she would still say, *'I want to stay with you,'* because deep inside, there was an insecurity which should never have been there, because of the interruption. Likewise, all kinds of things can sabotage our intimacy with God, affecting our ability to love ourselves well. This causes us insecurity, and in order for us to be re-connected later and reassured, God may need to teach us healthy new habits of self-care, even up to our old age!

If we are to love *ourselves* as well as *others*, then we need to know how to cherish ourselves; mind, body and spirit, and then, and only then, do we give – out of our Overflow. Those who are true martyrs, who sacrifice well, are those who are already rooted in love. It is only then that we are able to hear Jesus' words which encourage us to go the extra mile in loving others, without neglecting our own wholeness:

> *A new commandment I give to you, that you love one another; as I have loved you, that you also love one another. By this all will know that you are My disciples, if you have love for one another."* (John 13:34-35 NKJV)

To cherish ourselves is to love ourselves as God would have us loved. We want to get to the stage where we can overflow love and service to others, but we need to know how to strengthen *ourselves* in the Lord, how to encourage ourselves when we're isolated and how to protect ourselves when under spiritual attack. This spiritual cherishing is the most important, as it flows towards everything else. When our spirit is strengthened and encouraged, then our emotions and body come into alignment with it. This is why faith, hope and love are all important – as spiritual virtues; they are catalysts to everything else.

By establishing cherishing/self-care strategies, we are ensuring that we're in a place where we look after the Overflow from our spirit: where we're covered and protected.

So, living from the Overflow is one of the main ways that we protect what is necessary to our whole well-being from being stolen from by the enemy, and instead, keep in step with God's kingdom, naturally becoming immunised against the enemy's influences in the process.

Stop Working for God

I've met many who are over tired, over busy, distracted, discouraged and disheartened, all because they're NOT living from the Overflow, but instead are in survival mode. They're working for God, instead of with God. When we live in the Overflow, we work with God, led by His ways and His timing.

A while back, God asked me to give Him a whole day in my week. I already had a day off and then half a day which was for my family, so it would make two and a half days in my week that I would not be 'working'. I ummed and ahhed over whether or not I was hearing God rightly, but in the end, I did what He asked.

It was amazing! My quiet time with Him became truly intimate. I became connected to a flow of inspiration which seemed to come not from myself. Even sermon preparation and ideas started flowing so quickly, it saved me time. I actually got more done in less time. You could say it all happened because I'm more introverted. You could say that the lack of interruptions enabled me to stay focussed; but the truth is, instead of focussing on doing stuff *for* God, *dwelling with* God enabled me to marinate in His presence and then flow in the Spirit. Since that time, when God says *'Come away with Me'*, I'm off!

One of the things we need to learn, if we're going to live from the Overflow, is to prioritise and discipline our time. We may think we have no time, or too little time, but it is our time to take hold of. *We're the head, not the tail.* We can have our enthusiastic moments, when we want to 'give our all' to God, but when God challenges us about how we sometimes spend our time, are we willing to give up a certain thing?

Where we're not in control of our time, either because we're pressured by the expectations of others or ourselves, or we're pressured by fear or perfectionism, we are not prioritising those things that cherish our intimacy with God. The enemy has already stolen that from us. If we're going to take back our time and our destiny, then we need to sit up and recognise *who* God has called us to be, *what* He's asking us to do at this moment *in time*, and then *prioritise* it enough to just do it!

Anchored and Rooted in God

Imagine that you were wobbly on your feet, and at the same time you put out a hand to help someone else who was wobbly. You would both most likely fall over. But if you're secure and sturdy, then you can offer a hand that is secure and becomes like a solid rock to others.

Many of us try to help others when we're still wobbly ourselves, and we end up falling, or at the least, being dragged down, because we try and help from our own limited resources. We may even then miss other God-given priorities because we're not being Spirit-led.

When we live from the Overflow, not only are we sturdy and refreshing to be around, but what people get from us is *more* God and *less* us, because it's from the Overflow; it's anointing. It comes naturally, and half the time we won't know what we've said or done to encourage someone, but they will have been encouraged by the Overflow, the anointing that oozes from us.

When God is a priority in our life, we will be willing to let go of anything that is important to us because we love Him more and want to follow Him in every way. We should always want to defer to His wisdom and love, because He wants to protect us and love us, and not allow us to waste our lives and our time. He wants to restore what the enemy robs.

Anchored Lives Bring Peace

When we're living from a place of peace, we are no longer influenced by anger or fear in our hearts, and we are instead overflow-ers of peace. The Bible says:

> *'Blessed are the peacemakers, for they shall be called sons of God.'* (Matthew 5:9 NKJV)

What that means is, when we're walking in peace, the anointing from God that we carry will affect every situation we walk in.

No one likes fighting or war, even those who are propelled into it. No one loves the torment and the pain of disagreement, though it may seem that way at times. There may be some who find themselves in vicious circles, but in reality, they're stuck in torment and, like Legion who came to sit at Jesus' feet, compassion will be the one thing they will respond to.

I've discovered that most people who spout accusation from their mouths are being beaten up by the accuser on the inside and are un-cherished in how they operate. They're angry, unhappy people. When we're living from the Overflow, and connected in intimacy with God who exudes acceptance, rejection cannot possibly get a foothold. From this rooted, accepted place, living and breathing with Jesus, the Holy Spirit will challenge our fear, our inability to forgive and our inability to walk in peace such that gradually, we leave these things behind. When we're living from the Overflow, we leave a fragrance and a beauty behind us that brings peace, order and revelation – all good Kingdom stuff!

> *But the wisdom that is from above is first pure, then peaceable, gentle, willing to yield, full of mercy and good fruits, without partiality and without hypocrisy. Now the fruit of righteousness is sown in peace by those who make peace.* (James 3:17-18 NKJV)

When we're not living from the Overflow, the enemy has already stolen from us, because we have become disconnected from Jesus, the vine and our life-line.

> *Yes, I am the vine; you are the branches. Those who remain in me, and I in them, will produce much fruit. For apart from me you can do nothing. Anyone who does not remain in me is thrown away like a useless branch and withers. Such branches are gathered into a pile to be burned. But if you remain in me and my words remain in you, you may ask for anything you want, and it will be granted! When you produce much fruit, you are my true disciples. This brings great glory to my Father.* (John 15:5-8 NLT)

In other words, if we're not connected to Jesus – if we're not Spirit-led – then we're not living from the Overflow or producing good fruit in our lives. If we want to Take Back Who We Are In Christ, and live in Spirit-led opportunities that God gives, we *need* to live from the Overflow.

In summary, to get things spiritually balanced, our focus needs to start with intimacy with God, focussing on who He is and His abundant goodness. From this intimacy, we become recharged and re-aligned to His purposes, full of His love and His powerful presence. From this secure, rooted place, we naturally receive and give out of our abundance, not out of our left-overs or what we need for ourselves. The great thing is, the two most important commandments are then followed much better: we're responding to the Father's love better and recognising our need for it, and we're loving ourselves and others much better because we're overflowing. Then we become able to love like Jesus loves us.

Living From the Overflow

CHAPTER 5

Soul-Proofing

Our Influences and Jesus' Solution

How do we protect our minds, our will and our emotions from the spiritual assaults that life brings?

Well, firstly we need to know our Bible and what God says about us, as well as the spiritual world we live in. Knowing the Word and getting it deep inside us is fundamental to having revelation deep in our hearts.

The Bible says that the battle we are in, as Christians, is not with flesh and blood. In other words, it's not against people, though you wouldn't think that if you looked at the news, or if you're feeling bruised by someone at the moment. So let's get that point straight, it's a pretty huge point. Your feelings may say one thing, but the Bible says another – our war is not with people – full-stop.

Also, the Bible says that we are influenced by *'powers and principalities'* through our carnal desires. So, if we're going to protect ourselves against the assaults of what might be described as 'spiritual weather', then we need to understand how the enemy works in our heart and mind. We need to understand more about the spiritual world so we can position ourselves to be the head and not the tail.

> *What is causing the quarrels and fights among you? Don't they come from the evil desires at war within you? You want what you don't have, so you scheme and kill to get it. You are jealous of what others have, but you can't get it, so you fight and wage war to take it away from them. Yet you don't have what you want because you don't ask God for it.* (James 4:1-2 NLT)

> *I say then: Walk in the Spirit, and you shall not fulfill the lust of the flesh. For the flesh lusts against the Spirit, and the Spirit against the flesh; and these are contrary to one another, so that you do not do the things that you wish. But if you are led by the Spirit, you are not under the law.* (Galatians 5:16-18 NKJV)

Now, I used to say that I wanted to learn everything about healing, but I didn't want anything to do with the devil or deliverance (all that kind of talk around Christians made me a bit uncomfortable) – but it was a little bit ignorant of me, really, as the two are interconnected, whether I *like* it or not.

Jesus' Intention – Our Wholeness

Jesus made it clear that His agenda for us is fullness of life (or overflowing life!), but He also demonstrated the necessity of destroying the works of the evil one in order to enter into fullness, because the devil comes to steal from, kill and destroy us. If Jesus needed to destroy the works of the evil one, then how much more do we need to do that?

> *The thief does not come except to steal, and to kill, and to destroy. I have come that they may have life, and that they may have it more abundantly.* (John 10:10 NKJV)

It's true that the work that Jesus accomplished on the cross is complete: He took our sin (including our sickness and weakness) to the cross, and in exchange, offers forgiveness, healing and transformation. However, if we don't apply 'His blood' (the complete transforming reality of His sacrifice) to every part of our lives, then we won't be 'soul-proofed' everywhere; we'll be exposed in places and the enemy will take advantage of us through those areas.

It's a bit like scotch-guarding a tent or an anorak; if the rain-proofing has worn down or has never been there, then when it rains, the water just soaks through and you get wet every time. But with rain-proofing present, then it can rain constantly, yet you're still dry on the inside. We all know of Christian leaders who 'fell' and who ended up losing their whole ministry and often their families because they had not protected themselves against the enemy's wiles in a certain area of their life. We don't have to learn from mistakes by making them ourselves – let us learn from each others' mistakes also.

How the Enemy Robs Us

The enemy works in many different ways to rob us of overflowing life:

- He's a bully who uses fear to pressure us;
- He's a liar, but he'll use just enough truth about a situation to make us believe the lie;
- He's a deceiver, and in order to deceive, he keeps things hidden from us that we need to know to make the 'right' decision.
- He's corrupt and hides the real nature of God from us, for fear that we would come to know our place and take our place in God's family.

Thank God for the Holy Spirit who brings us the revelation we desperately need.

> *When the Spirit of truth comes, he will guide you into all truth.* (John 16:13a NLT)

How Temptation Works

When we're in the middle of being misled in our thoughts (maybe feeling we can't give something up e.g. a thought, a habit or a temptation), the way the enemy deceives us is to make us think that we *must indulge ourselves with it or we can't do without that particular thing and we're neglecting ourselves if we do.* The feelings he uses are seemingly irresistible at the time and blind us from the full consequences of our actions.

The enemy knows our carnal desires (lusts and urges for things) and will plant these thoughts in our minds that are not true, like *'you can't live without this',* then when we act on that thought, that action will give him permission to come and take a stronghold in our lives in that area. For instance: *'So-and-so doesn't care about me.'* If that's a thought that he plants, and we believe it, then our whole life will take on a pattern that will demonstrate that that is true. Growing up, I believed a lie that I wasn't intellectual, so I didn't even apply for university initially, because I was convinced that the lie was truth. Silly me! What we believe guides our decisions. Still, God has had the last laugh now, as I exposed the lie and acted on the truth. I'll go on to explain more about this in the next chapter, but suffice it to say that if we *believe a lie*, then we will *act* on the lie and therefore *empower* the enemy. *We empower what we believe.*

So, to start Taking Back, it is fundamentally important to develop a mindset that listens to God, others and ourselves well, so that we can examine our beliefs and root out the lies. Ungodly beliefs are the way that the enemy gains access into our minds and spirits, and when we believe these, we empower the enemy to create a stronghold in us.

As soon as we believe a lie or truth, we're beginning to act on it already, because we're *choosing to view life through that filter.* Acting on it is therefore imminent.

When we choose to believe the truth that God says about us, there will be an opportunity to act on the *truth* rather than the lie.

> *No temptation has overtaken you except such as is common to man; but* ***God is faithful, who will not allow you to be tempted beyond what you are able, but with the temptation will also make the way of escape****, that you may be able to bear it.*
> (1 Corinthians 10:13 NKJV)

Proofing Our Soul

You see, we always have a choice. Whenever there's an un-godly belief, there's a godly truth to counter it. For example:

> *'I can't possibly do this!'* is countered by

> *'I can do all things through Christ who strengthens me.*
> (Philippians 4:13 NKJV)

The way that we 'proof' our soul is to replace the lies (about ourselves, God or others) with Bible-based, Holy Spirit-inspired truth, and to recognise and kick out those strongholds that have naturally permeated and become part of our lives, such as rejection, fear or accusation.

How do you recognise if you have any of these? Well, if I walk into a room and you don't talk to me for any reason, and I'm carrying rejection, then I may feel hurt, believing you are rejecting me for some reason. I could be offended by your not recognising me. If I didn't carry rejection, then I might just think, *'Oh, they're busy,'* and not take anything personally.

> *But God showed his great love for us by sending Christ to die for us while we were still sinners. And since we have been made right in God's sight by the blood*

> *of Christ, he will certainly save us from God's condemnation. For since our friendship with God was restored by the death of his Son while we were still his enemies, we will certainly be saved through the life of his Son.* (Romans 5:8-10 NKJV)

If fear had a stronghold in me, and somebody did not turn up to an appointment, I might get all panicky and confused, and convinced that the person who has not shown up has had an accident, rather than see the bigger picture and think clearly. There is a reason why angels said *'Do not fear'* as soon as they appeared to God's people in the Bible – so that people saw and heard clearly what was being said, rather than letting fear rob them of hearing God's word clearly. We're not designed to carry fear into tomorrow:

> *Therefore do not worry about tomorrow, for tomorrow will worry about its own things. Sufficient for the day is its own trouble.* (Matthew 6:34 NKJV)

If accusation was a part of my life, and the enemy had a stronghold in me in that area, then criticism and judging would be natural for me in the way that I looked at life, myself and others. It's like a negative lens that colours perception, robbing us of a Kingdom outlook.

> *Do not judge others, and you will not be judged. Do not condemn others, or it will all come back against you. Forgive others, and you will be forgiven.* (Luke 6:37 NLT)
>
> *...in the last days perilous times will come: For men will be lovers of themselves, lovers of money, boasters, proud, blasphemers, disobedient to parents, unthankful, unholy, unloving, unforgiving, slanderers, without self-control, brutal, despisers of good, traitors,*

headstrong, haughty, lovers of pleasure rather than lovers of God, having a form of godliness but denying its power. And from such people turn away! (2 Timothy 3:1-5 NKJV)

If bitterness had a hold of me, then I would easily get angry with people, or maybe I would describe it as getting *frustrated* a lot. We're not designed to carry these things and they have a negative impact on our soul and bodies. There's a reason the Bible suggests we don't let anger settle on us for more than a day.

Get rid of all bitterness, rage, anger, harsh words, and slander, as well as all types of evil behaviour. (Ephesians 4:31 NLT)

If I had all these different things (and more!) working as my filters, you can see how hard it might be to have an anchored sense of peace and clear leading of the Holy Spirit! Even if we try and gloss over the negative thoughts in our heads with a Christian slant, the stronghold is still there.

The enemy can gain access into our minds, altering our mindsets by the un-godly beliefs he plants, and then he builds a stronghold in us that becomes part of us. That's when we think it is *us* who is the source of these thoughts; we fail to recognise it's the *enemy in us* instead. Let me be clear: when we have a stronghold, it's actually the enemy who has become rooted in us (because we've believed his lies). I know this because I used to have pretty much all these strongholds in my life and I am now mostly free.

The enemy knows the carnal lusts and desires we struggle with, and whilst we are not the source, we have become joined to that source. The enemy knows the things with which he can tempt us. He also knows our history with temptation, because he authored it!

> *Let no one say when he is tempted, "I am tempted by God"; for God cannot be tempted by evil, nor does He Himself tempt anyone. But each one is tempted when he is drawn away by his own desires and enticed. Then, when desire has conceived, it gives birth to sin; and sin, when it is full-grown, brings forth death.* (James 1:13-15 NKJV)

I recognised I had all kinds of issues when I was younger, but what I didn't realise was that those thoughts didn't originate in me; they had come in to nest, they were an infestation. However, gradually, as I replaced the lies with God's truth, I pushed back the enemy's hold in my life to Take Hold Of Who I Am In Christ, and who God created me to be. My mind is now calm and still and I enjoy a positive mental health – very unlike what it used to be. The Good News is, I can now help other people when they struggle with the same problems; I can identify signs of the enemy's hold over people's minds.

> *Blessed is the man who endures temptation; for when he has been approved, he will receive the crown of life which the Lord has promised to those who love Him* (James 1:12 NKJV)

Being Thorough

Many Christians try and overshadow their strongholds with truth (like many people who 'manage' their issues. I'm not into Anger Management, but anger elimination!).

What happens is that their strongholds are still there (albeit hiding), and in our 'not-so-nice-moments', they can just pop their heads up above our polite Christian veneer. Please hear me clearly: there's no shame in dealing thoroughly with 'nits'! We should always be watchful of our heart and will do much better to bring these things to Jesus for thorough sorting, instead of hiding them out of fear, so that we don't miss an essential place that needs de-cluttering and cleansing.

> *The heart is deceitful above all things, and desperately wicked; who can know it? I, the Lord, search the heart, I test the mind, even to give every man according to his ways, according to the fruit of his doings.*
> (Jeremiah 17:9-10 NKJV)

I wrote a book on forgiveness two years ago, and last year when at *Catch The Fire* in Toronto, I found myself being prayed for by Duncan Smith for car crash injuries. He asked if I had forgiven the driver who caused the accident I was in 20 years ago. I had, but I followed his prayer anyway, as I didn't want to cause embarrassment to anyone by saying otherwise. When I came down from the stage however, the Spirit reminded me of a friend who had implied my accident was caused by my disobedience. (I had sang the Messiah in Constitution Hall the night before my accident with a Christian Performing Arts Group but it took some time to get my breastfed youngest onto a bottle in time for the event – my friend had thought I should not have sung and that the difficulty I had experienced was evidence of it not being God's will). I thought I had forgiven her for her thoughtless words, but I remembered I still carried a bit of offence, as I had repeated the story to someone recently. So, in remembering that I still 'remembered' enough to repeat it, I forgave her and myself, and thanked God for the rather strange way that He reminded me. We can never be too forgiving, but this does not mean that we have to let people hurt us again and again.

Another reason why it's best to deal with these things properly is because the Kingdom virtue, which Jesus wants reigning where our stronghold resides, will find it impossible to grow roots all the time that the space is already occupied. There is, in reality, still a stronghold in the rightful place where Kingdom stuff should grow.

So we need to really cast stuff away from us, not just shove it into a closet and hope no one goes there.

> *Therefore submit to God. Resist the devil and he will flee from you.* (James 4:7 NKJV)

> *For God is working in you, giving you the desire and the power to do what pleases him.* (Philippians 2:13 NLT)

Enduring Opposition

There may be times when we are overwhelmed by spiritual attack, like Elijah who was hunted by Jezebel, or like David, when Saul was trying to kill him. We have a choice, even in difficult circumstances, whether to be ruled by fear, like Saul was, or to be ruled by trust in God, which David demonstrated, even against the odds. Note the two very different fruit and destinations that Saul and David inherited, based on what thoughts they acted on.

> *One day near Horesh, David received the news that Saul was on the way to Ziph to search for him and kill him. Jonathan went to find David and encouraged him to stay strong in his faith in God. "Don't be afraid," Jonathan reassured him. "My father will never find you! You are going to be the king of Israel, and I will be next to you, as my father, Saul, is well aware." So the two of them renewed their solemn pact before the Lord. Then Jonathan returned home, while David stayed at Horesh* (1 Samuel 23: 15-18 NLT)

God knows that our hearts can become weak within us under immense opposition, not necessarily because we lack courage, but because the battle may be ongoing, and we become worn down, emotionally and spiritually. God designed for there to be a way out for us, a strengthening process ahead of time. For David, he was encouraged by Jonathan, who pacified his very real fears.

In Hebrews, we are commanded to have a covering attitude towards each other, *helping to be each other's advocate in order to strengthen each other in the Lord:* this godly attribute is very dear to God's heart:

> *Be careful then, dear brothers and sisters. Make sure that your own hearts are not evil and unbelieving, turning you away from the living God.* ***You must warn each other every day, while it is still "today," so that none of you will be deceived by sin and hardened against God.*** (Hebrews 3:12-13 NLT)

> *But he (Elijah) himself went a day's journey into the wilderness, and came and sat down under a broom tree. And he prayed that he might die, and said, "It is enough! Now, Lord, take my life, for I am no better than my fathers!" Then as he lay and slept under a broom tree, suddenly an angel touched him, and said to him, "Arise and eat." Then he looked, and there by his head was a cake baked on coals, and a jar of water. So he ate and drank, and lay down again. And the angel of the Lord came back the second time, and touched him, and said, "Arise and eat, because the journey is too great for you." So he arose, and ate and drank; and he went in the strength of that food forty days and forty nights as far as Horeb, the mountain of God. And there*

he went into a cave, and spent the night in that place; and behold, the word of the Lord came to him, and He said to him, "What are you doing here, Elijah?" So he said, "I have been very zealous for the Lord God of hosts; for the children of Israel have forsaken Your covenant, torn down Your altars, and killed Your prophets with the sword. I alone am left; and they seek to take my life."

Then He said, "Go out, and stand on the mountain before the Lord." And behold, the Lord passed by, and a great and strong wind tore into the mountains and broke the rocks in pieces before the Lord, but the Lord was not in the wind; and after the wind an earthquake, but the Lord was not in the earthquake; and after the earthquake a fire, but the Lord was not in the fire; and after the fire a still small voice. (1 Kings 19:4-12 NKJV)

When Elijah was going through it, there wasn't anyone around who could understand his situation, so God spoke to Elijah himself and sent an angel to strengthen him, for the Lord does not want our heart to be overwhelmed with discouragement.

Once we have discovered how to strengthen ourselves and protect our weaknesses, then we need to get boundaries or processes in place to protect the ground that has been regained, else it will be retaken again. I talk about this in another chapter, but here is an example which demonstrates the enemy's strategy:

When I carried rejection, I used to find that the enemy would plant accusing thoughts in my mind about what others thought about me. Once I realised his strategy, I made it *a principle to dismiss any thought that was negative without clear evidence* – I would just ignore such thoughts immediately and recognised them as a mixture of rejection and paranoia. I now find that these thoughts don't come knocking any more. This is an example of a boundary process I created, which prevents the enemy robbing me of my peace and self-worth.

So, to summarise, if we're going to soul-proof ourselves against the enemy, we need to *believe the truth that God says about us (in every respect) and we need to replace the lies which are from the enemy with divine truth.*

So we need to have our L-plates on permanently this side of heaven, until we have got rid of every stronghold in our lives, until we are so full of Who We Are In Christ that we don't see the enemy's hand in our lives anymore. In that way, we are protecting ourselves from the enemy taking any more of our lives, and allowing God instead to have the freehold in our lives instead.

> *"Success is not measured by what you accomplish, but by the opposition you have encountered, and the courage with which you have maintained the struggle against overwhelming odds."* (Orison Swett Marden)

Soul-Proofing

CHAPTER 6

Dying Well

He went on a little farther and bowed with his face to the ground, praying, "My Father! If it is possible, let this cup of suffering be taken away from me. ***Yet I want your will to be done, not mine.****"* (Matthew 26:39 NLT)

All changes, even the most longed for, have their melancholy; for what we leave behind us is part of ourselves; ***we must die to one life before we can enter another.*** (Anatole France.)

When we are first touched by God's love, when we come to know Him, we realise that many passions and desires that have become part of our lives aren't meant to be part of Who We Are In Christ. There are unique things that are meant to stay, and also things which do not make God smile. There's a list in Galatians 5 that talks about the fruits of the Spirit, but just prior of that list, there are things we're encouraged to get rid of in order to embrace these fruits of the Spirit, e.g. anger. A bit like a de-clutter before a good deep clean!

So I say, let the Holy Spirit guide your lives. Then you won't be doing what your sinful nature craves. The sinful nature wants to do evil, which is just the opposite of what the Spirit wants. And the Spirit gives us desires that are the opposite of what the sinful nature desires. These two forces are constantly fighting each other, so you are not free to carry out your good intentions.

> *But when you are directed by the Spirit, you are not under obligation to the law of Moses. When you follow the desires of your sinful nature, the results are very clear: sexual immorality, impurity, lustful pleasures, idolatry, sorcery, hostility, quarrelling, jealousy, outbursts of anger, selfish ambition, dissension, division, envy, drunkenness, wild parties, and other sins like these. Let me tell you again, as I have before, that anyone living that sort of life will not inherit the Kingdom of God.*
>
> *But the Holy Spirit produces this kind of fruit in our lives: love, joy, peace, patience, kindness, goodness, faithfulness, gentleness, and self-control. There is no law against these things! Those who belong to Christ Jesus have nailed the passions and desires of their sinful nature to his cross and crucified them there. Since we are living by the Spirit, let us follow the Spirit's leading in every part of our lives.* (Galatians 5:16-25 NLT)

We are told to get rid of the things in our lives which will affect the Holy Spirit being 'at home' in us, becoming rooted in us. But these things only go as we 'die' to them, and I've discovered that it's fundamentally important that we learn how to 'die' well.

> *Well then, should we keep on sinning so that God can show us more and more of his wonderful grace? Of course not! Since we have died to sin, how can we continue to live in it? Or have you forgotten that when we were joined with Christ Jesus in baptism, we joined him in his death?* (Romans 6:1-3 NLT)

If we want to see blessing, fruit, resurrection, transformation, etc. in our lives, then we need to die to those things which stand in the way, and we'll need to die completely! Sometimes when

I'm listening to people talk about sacrifices they have made, they are still waiting for the reward - and they've sacrificed for years! But it becomes apparent to me that they haven't yet died properly. God knows our hearts. I know it's a strange phrase, but Jesus used it, and what He said was *'deny yourself, follow me, pick up your cross.'* In another place, Paul talks about 'dying daily,' and being crucified with Christ.

> *I affirm, by the boasting in you which I have in Christ Jesus our Lord,* ***I die daily.*** *Awake to righteousness, and do not sin; for some do not have the knowledge of God.* (1 Corinthians 15:31, 34)
>
> *Therefore, dear brothers and sisters, you have no obligation to do what your sinful nature urges you to do. For if you live by its dictates, you will die. But* ***if through the power of the Spirit you put to death the deeds of your sinful nature, you will live.*** *For all who are led by the Spirit of God are children of God. So you have not received a spirit that makes you fearful slaves. Instead, you received God's Spirit when he adopted you as his own children. Now we call him, "Abba, Father." For his Spirit joins with our spirit to affirm that we are God's children. And since we are his children, we are his heirs. In fact, together with Christ we are heirs of God's glory. But if we are to share his glory, we must also share his suffering.* (Romans 8:12-17 NLT)

Understanding Lust

Anything that is bigger in our lives than God (people, money, desires, etc.) needs to die, because of its hold and influence on us, before we're able to experience those same things in a Kingdom way.

> *Then Jesus said to His disciples, "If anyone desires to come after Me, let him deny himself, and take up his cross, and follow Me. For whoever desires to save his life will lose it, but whoever loses his life for My sake will find it. For what profit is it to a man if he gains the whole world, and loses his own soul? Or what will a man give in exchange for his soul?"* (Matthew 16:24-25)

Those things, that would otherwise pull us away from the Kingdom of God, need to be defined by God, not shaped by ourselves.

> *So you also should consider yourselves to be dead to the power of sin and alive to God through Christ Jesus. Do not let sin control the way you live; do not give in to sinful desires. Do not let any part of your body become an instrument of evil to serve sin. Instead, give yourselves completely to God, for you were dead, but now you have new life. So use your whole body as an instrument to do what is right for the glory of God.* (Romans 6:11-13 NLT)

If we are to die well, we need to crucify that anger, that lust, that thing we're wanting more than we want God. The reason God hates idols, as we see in both the Old and New Testament, is because they stand in the place of Him.

After my first marriage ended, I was convinced I never wanted to remarry. Whoever has been through a difficult marriage break-up carries a degree fear and failure. Yet when Jasper came along, I felt my heart re-awaken, and before long, I found myself dreaming of being with him. I had received two prophetic words confirming that I would end up with him, but there were still times when I had to 'die' to the idea of being with him, because of how big he became in my focus at that time. In my lonely times, my longing for him was greater than my longing for God. I never want anything or anyone to take the place of God in my life, so I died to being with Jasper, so that even if we didn't end up together, that was OK in my spirit with me. I must have died well, as I've been married to him five and a half years now.

Years ago, God miraculously cured a friend, Tina, through healing prayer in ICU, but first, the Lord asked me to challenge her husband that if it was her time, was he willing to let her go? He was, but God healed her miraculously anyway, and because of the challenge, strengthened his relationship with God. He died to being with his wife.

I talked to a new friend who described how God asked her to give up her well paid professional job, which she did, but then He asked her to give away her last wage completely. She was surprised, but did as she was asked. Within a day, she had received more in a gift than her wage was. God was wanting to make sure she became more reliant on His grace than her money. She died to being in control of her finances.

When the Bible talks about lust, most of us just think of sexual lust, but lust means 'I want what I want, and I want it now, in the way I want.' This could apply to many different things, for example: I may want a cream cake, and if I want it now, then I will just use my money and time to go and buy one and eat it. However, if God is going to be the master of my time, my money and my priorities, then my priorities and time need to be shaped by God. I can't allow my timing or priorities to dictate my life, because my life is no longer my own.

If I want what I want, and I want it now, then I have to recognise it as lust and I need to recognise the feeling inside of me, so that I can keep it in check. It's a carnal desire, the Bible says, and it's going to stand in the way of transformation and God's blessing on my life. When we get things that we want through lust, it's like we get a half empty glass of water of poor quality, rather than an overflowing glass of best quality.

If lust is rooted in our lives, then the enemy has already blinded us and tripped us up. He has stopped us getting blessing in that area of our lives, so we need to die to that lust in order to experience the godly equivalent. Lust is a very poor counterfeit of the real thing; so we may want to be loved, but if we're lusting to be loved, and we can't control that lust, we may go from one relationship to another, feeling totally rejected and get disappointed time after time. But if we crucify that lust and give it to God again and again, making *Him* our first love, then God will give us the person of our dreams, in His time and His way, when the lust in us has finally died. His timing is perfect. He Himself said that it's not good for man to be alone, so if we say to Him *'I'm lonely and I really would love someone'*, then He knows that we need someone, and it will become part of His plan for us. We *must* crucify our lusts though, *really* dying to them in order to allow God to work in our lives, because the sooner we die to these things, the sooner blessings will come in these areas.

> *Since you have heard about Jesus and have learned the truth that comes from him, throw off your old sinful nature and your former way of life, which is corrupted by lust and deception. Instead, let the Spirit renew your thoughts and attitudes. Put on your new nature, created to be like God – truly righteous and holy.* (Ephesians 4:21-24 NLT)

Where Lust Shapes a Need

You know, some of the things that we may be wanting are needs, such as food to eat, or petrol to put in the car to get to work, etc. Necessities are different to lusts, though if I need a sofa, and only a very expensive sofa will do, then that may well be a lust.

Years ago, I was needing a sideboard, as I was hosting a Bible study group and wanting something to store toys in for the group's children. I prayed for a sideboard, and it didn't come. I asked some more, and it didn't come. In the end, I went to Marks and Spencers and bought a sideboard for £750, to be paid off a little bit at a time over the next year. Two days later, there were two sideboards that were absolutely perfect in the local paper for about £25 each. I was spitting feathers. I was so mad! I went to see them, feeling repentant in my heart for not trusting God to provide and sorrowful that that I hadn't waited just that little bit longer, and that the enemy had just taken my money for the next year, when he needn't have done if I had just waited. I was contracted for a year to pay off this sideboard I'd bought impatiently (which I've now given to someone else, by the way), but I bought these two other sideboards that were in the paper as well. They were part of our family life for many years, and I had bought them as a reminder that when I'm feeling impatient, blessing is just round the corner. I hadn't died enough to my impatience at that point in my life.

> *So don't worry about these things, saying, 'What will we eat? What will we drink? What will we wear?' These things dominate the thoughts of unbelievers, but your heavenly Father already knows all your needs.* ***Seek the Kingdom of God above all else, and live righteously, and he will give you everything you need.*** (Matthew 6:31-33 NKJV)

Keeping Your Heart True as You Die

When I first moved to Sheffield and was living by faith financially, someone had asked me to pick up a cake to deliver to someone, and when I arrived to pick up the cake, I found it on the doorstep. Next to it was a baked potato wrapped in tin foil, with a note saying *'I've made you a baked potato, I know how you like them.'* I was quite devastated, because while my initial thoughts were of gratitude, I remembered that I didn't even have any butter in the cupboards to put on it, and I had no filling for it. There were lots of 'buts' that came into my mind, and the Lord rebuked me and said:

'Give thanks for what you've got, you've got a car to take this cake to where it needs to go, and you have a baked potato, so start thanking me.'

I recognised that my attitude was wrong; I needed to die to ingratitude, as my heart was all wrong. So I started thanking God for the cold baked potato, and I thanked God that I had some salt to put on it when I got home, and then I started to thank God for other things, and found that my attitude started to change. Within a few days, I had been invited out for two different meals! Also, my small group had a group meal, and everyone took £5 to contribute towards the food. For me, £5 was money that I hadn't got, but I turned up at the group, and was going to give the £5 that would normally have lasted me the week. As I arrived, the host collected everyone's money and just put it all into my pocket. God's provision! I almost didn't go that night, but I knew God was in it, and I didn't let my pitiful contribution and unthankful heart stand in the way of God's blessings, which exceeded my expectations.

God-Shaped Perspective

You see, when God doesn't have the first place in the whole of our lives, then our perspective can be skewed, like an orphan, and we are mean-sighted. Like those mirrors at the fairground, or the wrong pair of glasses, we're not seeing right, and we see God and others in a poor light. And so, every decision we make with a wrong perspective will be influenced by that wrong perspective.

When we die to our human way of operating, then blessing comes quicker. When my marriage failed and I had two people (besides myself) who I needed to forgive, I said to God:

'You have to show me how to forgive quickly because I can't stand up there, in front of the church every week, forgiving other people's sin and telling people to forgive other people's sin if I can't forgive.'

Everyone told me it would be 4-5 years before I'd even be ready for another relationship, but there was no way I was putting my ministry on hold for 5 years, as I had already felt robbed. So I determined to die as quickly as I could. God helped me enormously, showing me that sin is blind, and it became easier for me to forgive quickly.

I don't know about you, but I want to just be influenced by the Lord, by the Holy Spirit. I want my perspective to be right. When we get rid of lusts (like anger) and issues that cause us to want things more than God, we begin to get godly desires instead. Those godly desires are birthed through the Holy Spirit; they're Kingdom desires, and they're always what we want, but so much more than what we could want, need, or expect, because God always blesses us more.

> *That is what the Scriptures mean when they say, "No eye has seen, no ear has heard, and* ***no mind has imagined what God has prepared for those who love him.****"*
> (1 Corinthians 2: 9 NLT)

For example, I could say *'Lord, I would love it if you provided my lunch today,'* and in doing so, God might actually provide a banquet to feed the five thousand, because *that's* the way He thinks. He's not just going to bless me, but He's going to bless me in such a way that there's an *overflow to others also*. Our perspective is muted where our lusts and desires have shaped our mindset. Lusts and passions and desires make us small minded and selfish, and in fact only serve the enemy's kingdom.

I love cream cakes, my daughters will tell you; if there's a strawberry cream tart somewhere nearby, then I will happily make a beeline for it, but since my recent 40 day fast, I made a decision with the Holy Spirit that I would pray about the things that I eat. I want food not to have a hold on me, and I want to stay dead in this area. And so, there have been several times since, when a strawberry tart, or something even nicer, has been beckoning me. But since I've spent the time to pray about the choice, He's not yet showed me a strawberry cream tart, so I've not eaten one. That may sound a bit extreme to you, but it's my decision based on my need, because I want to die to food having a hold on me. I want to be Spirit-led about everything.

Where God fills our perspective more than something else we may want, then we can enjoy all the things in life. But where something else is bigger than God (for some people it's food, for other it's relationships, for others it's addiction, etc.), those things need to be crucified. We need to die to things having a hold on us if we want to take back the ground the enemy has stolen from us. Where the enemy occupies an area in us, we will see the fruit of that, and it won't be good fruit. Where we take back that ground, and we give that ground to God instead, we get rid of that bad fruit, and what is planted instead bears fruit that is not only a blessing to us, but it's a blessing to other people as well.

Sometimes we need to die to things that are not sins, but in doing so, there will be a great reward. Mary, the mother of Jesus, died to her agenda and reputation, and in doing so, the

Lord's agenda was glorified and Mary's reputation later was given the honour it deserved.

Christ bids us: come and die. (Dietrich Bonhoeffer)

Dietrich Bonhoeffer became a living example of the above words. He ministered in England and Germany at a time it was not safe to do so, during the Second World War. He stood up for truth at a time when many leaders in the German church did not, because of fear and intimidation. Dietrich denounced Hitler's leadership in both words and actions, and was arrested in 1943. Two years later, he was hanged. He was martyred for Christ, and his sacrifice is still remembered today.

How humbling it is that people like him are willing to *literally* die to what they want, in order to bring the transformation of the Kingdom? Their reward really will be outstanding in heaven!

Dying Well

CHAPTER 7

Life in Fullness

"For everyone who asks receives, and he who seeks finds, and to him who knocks it will be opened. If a son asks for bread from any father among you, will he give him a stone? Or if he asks for a fish, will he give him a serpent instead of a fish? Or if he asks for an egg, will he offer him a scorpion? If you then, being evil, know how to give good gifts to your children, how much more will your heavenly Father give the Holy Spirit to those who ask Him!" (Luke 11:10-12 NKJV)

Many of us were sold a lie and are living a lie by believing that the Christian life is all about suffering. Yes, suffering is part of life, and Jesus said '*when* you have tribulation' not '*if* you have tribulation'.

But suffering is only half of the gospel. I lived a good 20 years of my early Christian life based on this lie, so I settled for less. When I developed Rheumatoid Arthritis, I learnt how to rejoice in suffering, but I know it was never God's will to afflict me, or for me to have lived outside of His protection (see Deuteronomy 28-30 if you don't believe me). I didn't think so at the time, but to be honest, I had a strong poverty spirit and a huge load of self-bitterness, so I was grateful for anything.

When I first had a miracle in my life, I was encouraged *not* to share it with others, as it was 'not fair' because other people still struggled in that area. What tosh! What a poverty-driven, mean mindset! That is not Jesus or fullness; that is fear, religion and an orphan mindset shaped by a poverty heart and jealousy.

The Progression from Suffering

The suffering cross enabled resurrection to new life!

Jesus set the oppressed free then and still does so today!

God still heals and raises the dead today!

That is the *other* side to the gospel – the one of hope, freedom and resurrection!

I love Jesus' response when the disciples got all excited about the freedom they were bringing to others in Jesus name.

> *'Rejoice not that the demons obey you. Rather rejoice that your names are written in the book of life.'* (Luke 10:20 NKJV)

You see, Jesus knew those things that were most important. And whilst most of those disciples sent the enemy packing their whole ministry life, all but one came to a persecuted sticky end. Instead of their dying breath calling out *'why'* to God, they were able to remember Jesus words, *'rejoice…that your names are written in the book of life'*. What a thought to hang on to as you go from this life to glory!

You see, life in all its fullness may have its suffering side, but it's not all sorrow – look at the pain of childbirth, and yet the rewards bring much joy. We are to focus on the important things in life, so let's not settle for less than Jesus died for. I personally want His sacrifice for me to be worth it, to bring Him much joy as He looks at my life. What about you?

This chapter is about challenging poverty mindsets, blowing the door right off the hinges so we can let the glory of God's marvellous plans speak for themselves. Fullness of life!

Knowing God

> *For the Lord God is a sun and shield; the Lord will give grace and glory; no good thing will He withhold from those who walk uprightly.* (Psalm 84:11 NKJV)

The God who calls you is mighty, holy and awesome, as well as gentle, intimate, and *so for you!* He's not a teddy or a lamb though – He's a lion with a tough roar for justice. He's a Father who wants to protect us from evil. He's a Mother (?!) who wants to nurture and encourage us. The Names of God (who He is) are many, and in every way that *He is*, He wants us to know Him.

You may feel unworthy at times – but He died for you and wants to bless your socks off! So remind yourself of this truth. You may feel ambivalent occasionally – so what? You may feel overwhelmed by life and circumstances, but He cares and wants to help. You may doubt, struggle with His philosophy, or kick against the goad, but it won't stop Him loving you and working in your life to see you overflowing. He loves you, and an intimate relationship with you is why He is chasing you.

When I was first called into ministry in 1993, I had a Damascus Road experience. In the middle of praying for the nations with a prayer ministry team at New Wine in Shepton Mallet, I was suddenly transported to the foot of the cross, and saw Jesus' broken body bleeding for me, from His side. At the same time, waves and waves of heavy ecstasy rolled over me until I thought I couldn't take any more. I felt like God came and sat on me! At which point, I saw clear words appear before my eyes:

I have sent you to declare My Name to the nations,
I have sent you to declare My Power to the nations,
I have sent you to declare My Love to the nations.
Go and do it.

I came to and realised God had spoken, though I still asked for confirmation through a person. Strange, I know! The next morning, the worship group 'Flamme' gave the identical prophecy, word for word, during the middle of the worship time.

Up until that point, I had internally ridiculed people who had 'so-called' prophetic words.

Up until that point, I had felt my past marriage problems had disqualified me from being as effective as I could be for God. Up until that point, I had felt extremely isolated and deemed 'unsuitable' for ministry, because of my many issues and wounds. Up until that point, I agreed with the many thoughts in my head that wanted to subdue and belittle me. No more. God spoke, He called, and that was the end of it.

I couldn't understand His reasoning, or why He should possibly choose me. I always seemed to put my foot in my mouth, and even I didn't choose me. But God did, and that was the end of it for me in my heart. It just took a while to filter through my mind.

- Knowing God really changes our heart and opens it to receive the love and fullness God has for us.
- Knowing God doesn't come from another person's experience of God.
- Knowing God doesn't come from reading the best books or testimonies.
- Knowing God doesn't come from education, or attending the best seminars or churches.
- Knowing God doesn't come from having the perfect family or perfect life.
- Knowing God doesn't come from knowing your Bible inside out or being religious.
- Knowing God comes from being touched by His love, His acceptance, and His call on your life. It's called 'revelation-knowledge', and anything that we do that

doesn't come from God will not be 'whole truth' and will come to nothing.

If we are to know God, we need to experience His love first-hand for ourselves, and keep doing so. This is key to Taking Back What The Enemy Has Stolen.

Know True Treasure

Jesus replied, "Friend, who made me a judge over you to decide such things as that?" Then he said, "Beware! Guard against every kind of greed. Life is not measured by how much you own." Then he told them a story: "A rich man had a fertile farm that produced fine crops. He said to himself, 'What should I do? I don't have room for all my crops.' Then he said, 'I know! I'll tear down my barns and build bigger ones. Then I'll have room enough to store all my wheat and other goods. And I'll sit back and say to myself, "My friend, you have enough stored away for years to come. Now take it easy! Eat, drink, and be merry!'

"But God said to him, 'You fool! You will die this very night. Then who will get everything you worked for?'

"Yes, a person is a fool to store up earthly wealth but not have a rich relationship with God."
(Luke 12:14-21 NLT)

Money can't buy anyone love or happiness, we all agree. The rich man was really not happy. He was insecure and only felt a degree of peace from his riches – riches were his security, but what a poor security they were. Riches couldn't bring health or extend his life. Riches don't make us open-hearted or give us true friends.

It's not that money is the issue – it's just that we give riches an importance and status that is undeserving. Like an idol, money is powerless to help us – it's just a vehicle. Nothing more. It doesn't come with a download of happiness.

Some wise person said:

> *Anyone who thinks money can buy happiness hasn't really got any.*

Another wise person said:

> *The blessing of the Lord makes a person rich, and he adds no sorrow with it.* (Proverbs 10:22 NLT)

Solomon (co-author of Proverbs) knew that riches are a heavy weight and responsibility, unless they come through God. God's riches, unlike worldly riches, are a blessing and not burdensome. Jesus' yoke is easy.

God is our true treasure and the Giver behind the gifts; the author of all good things; the One who cares for us, equips us with the wisdom we need, and transforms us into Who We Are In Christ. What a treasure! You can keep your money, give me God any day!

Use Your Resources

I have met many, many Christians who believe that we're most humble when we are poor; that we're meek when we're trodden on, and that 'making do' is what you do when you live by faith.

I have to say that this is entirely unbiblical! But it's taken me a long time to realise that! God's people may have to struggle by being called to dry, oppressed places to see transformation, but we're the head and not the tail! Look at all the promised blessings for all who follow God and His ways:

If you fully obey the Lord your God and carefully keep all his commands that I am giving you today, the Lord your God will set you high above all the nations of the world. You will experience all these blessings if you obey the Lord your God:

Your towns and your fields will be blessed.

Your children and your crops will be blessed.

The offspring of your herds and flocks will be blessed.

Your fruit baskets and breadboards will be blessed.

Wherever you go and whatever you do, you will be blessed.

The Lord will conquer your enemies when they attack you. They will attack you from one direction, but they will scatter from you in seven!

The Lord will guarantee a blessing on everything you do and will fill your storehouses with grain.

The Lord your God will bless you in the land he is giving you.

If you obey the commands of the Lord your God and walk in his ways, the Lord will establish you as his holy people as he swore he would do. Then all the nations of the world will see that you are a people claimed by the Lord, and they will stand in awe of you.

The Lord will give you prosperity in the land he swore to your ancestors to give you, blessing you with many children, numerous livestock, and abundant crops.

The Lord will send rain at the proper time from his rich treasury in the heavens and will bless all the work you do.

You will lend to many nations, but you will never need to borrow from them.

If you listen to these commands of the Lord your God that I am giving you today, and if you carefully obey them, the Lord will make you the head and not the tail, and you will always be on top and never at the bottom. You must not turn away from any of the commands I am giving you today, nor follow after other gods and worship them. (Deuteronomy 28:1-14 NLT)

This may not yet have been your experience, but this IS God's will for your life. Even if some of this makes you uncomfortable, remember, the Lord delights in you, and will bring His blessings to pass if you 'heed His commandments' and ways in every area of your life.

Every person who is born again is *supposed* to overcome the enemy and embrace fullness of life (see John 10:10).

If you look at every person who knew God in the Bible, they were not just blessed in their actions and relationships, but in their finances too!

The Bible doesn't say that money is the root of all evil – it says the LOVE of money is the root of all evil; placing our affection on things instead of the Provider of those things. It's the love of money that causes us to be attached to it.

And you shall **remember the LORD your God, for it is He who gives you power** *to get wealth, that He may establish His covenant which He swore to your fathers, as it is this day.* (Deuteronomy 8:18)

It's worth remembering that one of the ways we remember the Lord is by giving God the 'first fruits' of what He gives us. A tithe. It's like saying, *I'm aware that you are the One who gives me power to make (or get) wealth, and I want to honour you for that by giving you the first tenth (10%) and using the 90% for my own needs.* We're encouraged to give offerings (gifts of love) to people or ministries on top of that. In the New Testament, we're encouraged to give much more, but *cheerfully.*

I've heard it said you cannot out-give God. I truly believe it is true, and have tested this many times. If you are struggling financially, honour the Lord, honour your debts, love others (with *all* your resources), 'til it begins to be uncomfortable, and God will bless your socks off!

Remember: worldly things are fickle, so don't rely on them, but rely on God. Look at the story of Joseph: Jacob, his Dad, may have been wealthy, but it came to nothing in the drought. Joseph's wealth exceeded his father's in the end. He wasn't even looking for it! It came looking for him.

A good friend of mine called Trevor Newport says, *'I don't look for money. Money looks for me!'* That's because money has no spiritual hold on him, and the true riches of the Giver do have a hold on him.

Seek the Giver, not the gifts, and God will supply your needs amply. Ruth (a poor widow) ended up marrying Boaz, who was very wealthy, because she had God's heart for her mother-in-law and honoured her mother-in-law's wisdom.

> *There was a relative of Naomi's husband, a man of great wealth, of the family of Elimelech. His name was Boaz.* (Ruth 2:1 NLT)

Solomon's wealth was like no king's before or after him – because he asked for wisdom (spiritual treasure) and not money (worldly treasure). God knows that in order to steward money righteously, *you need wisdom first.* Once we get wisdom, money usually follows.

So God has no problem with money. But true riches are beyond any thing. Relationships, love, loyalty, respect and honour, a developed character, a life of love, wisdom.

Be a Son: Ask!

The difference between someone who thinks like an orphan and someone who thinks like a son is that someone who thinks like a son often thinks like a millionaire.

Sons are aware of the possible resources that are theirs in Christ, and therefore the creative potential that comes from anything being possible is 'loosed'.

Poverty thinking is typical of orphan hearts, who are not only stuck in their filtered thinking, but constrict and belittle others who take Jesus at His word, just because things haven't yet worked out for them.

This section is about helping us achieve the son mindset, to help us think bigger, and embrace our inheritance in Christ. We may never have thought this way, we may have always had a small mindset, we may have been born into it, or been shaped when we were younger, but those experiences don't have to limit us.

> *...you don't have what you want because you don't ask God for it.* (James 4:2b NLT)

> *And even when you ask, you don't get it because your motives are all wrong – you want only what will give you pleasure.* (James 4:3 NLT)

> *When you pray, don't babble on and on as people of other religions do. They think their prayers are answered merely by repeating their words again and again. Don't be like them, for your Father knows exactly what you need even before you ask him!* (Matthew 6:7-8 NLT)

> *Pray like this: Our Father in heaven, may your name be kept holy* (be honoured: my paraphrase!) *May your Kingdom come soon. May your will be done on earth, as it is in heaven.* (Matthew 6:9-10 NLT)
>
> *Don't worry about anything; instead, pray about everything. Tell God what you need, and thank him for all he has done. Then you will experience God's peace, which exceeds anything we can understand. His peace will guard your hearts and minds as you live in Christ Jesus.* (Philippians 4:6-8 NLT)

Fear and worry is not trusting God. If we don't trust Him with our needs, we won't ask Him for them. But He knows us and every need we have, and we honour Him by looking to Him for our needs – it's part of our being His children. He will honour us with a response, though His timing and ways of operating are not ours. He wants to stretch us, so that we recognise the fears we have and give them to Him. But it is worth the stretch, as He doesn't just supply our needs. He literally blesses our socks off!

> *And my God shall supply all your need according to His riches in glory by Christ Jesus.* (Philippians 4:19 NKJV)

God doesn't want to supply our needs (!) He wants to supply our needs *according to His riches in glory*. I know I've said this before, but it bears repeating!

I have many stories which illustrate this, but it would fill another book! Trust me when I say, that if you do as Jesus says below, you will not be disappointed.

> *Keep on asking, and you will receive what you ask for. Keep on seeking, and you will find. Keep on knocking, and the door will be opened to you. For everyone who asks, receives. Everyone who seeks, finds. And to everyone who knocks, the door will be opened.* (Matthew 7:6-8 NLT)

> *But know this, that in the last days perilous times will come: For men will be lovers of themselves, lovers of money, boasters, proud, blasphemers, disobedient to parents, unthankful, unholy, unloving, unforgiving, slanderers, without self-control, brutal, despisers of good, traitors, headstrong, haughty, lovers of pleasure rather than lovers of God, having a form of godliness but denying its power. And from such people turn away!* (2 Timothy 3:1-5 NKJV)

I remember reading this passage as a new Christian and thinking, *well that disqualifies me!* I had most of these issues and had no idea, at that point, that we could free ourselves from such things. So I felt very condemned and somewhat hopeless.

> *He gives us everything we need for life and for holy living. He gives it through His great power. As we come to know Him better, we learn that He called us to share His own shining-greatness and perfect life. Through His shining-greatness and perfect life, He has given us promises. These promises are of great worth and no amount of money can buy them. Through these promises you can have God's own life in you now that you have gotten away from the sinful things of the world which came from wrong desires of the flesh. Do your best to add holy living to your faith. Then add to this a better understanding. As you have a better understanding, be able to say no when you need to. Do not give up. And as you wait and do not give up, live God-like. As you live God-like, be kind to Christian*

brothers and love them. If you have all these things and keep growing in them, they will keep you from being of no use and from having no fruit when it comes to knowing our Lord Jesus Christ. (2 Peter 1:3-8 NLT)

All our filters (strongholds) will blind us to revelation that would increase our understanding and godly authority. So the more we get rid of them, the more we will both hear and operate like God.

If we can separate ourselves from our sin, mistakes, and weaknesses, it will be easier to forgive ourselves and receive God's unconditional love. That is the start of moving forward. Don't let shame, accusation and condemnation stand in the way of coming close to God. Those things come from the enemy and are not Kingdom feelings. They just show you which parts of you are not yet operating like a son.

One of the stumbling blocks to moving forward is self-pity. When we're having a 'pity party', stuck in a place of discouragement, we need to work on strengthening ourselves in the Lord. Recognise when you are in that place of negative discouraged thinking, and ask your loved ones to challenge you to look up at such times and prioritise cherishing your spirit.

Learn real, deep gratitude, and express it as often as you can. I had a church warden once, Paul Hope, who found it hard to sleep because he was worrying about his problems. I shared with him the song, *'When you're worried and you can't sleep, count your blessings instead of sheep, and you'll fall asleep counting your blessings.'*

Well, the next week I asked him how he got on. He said, *'I started counting my blessings and found I got more and more happy that in the end, I couldn't sleep 'cos I was so happy!'*

Free Thinking

As an orphan I'll think small, and I want to think like a millionaire, but not just to do with money. The Bible says *'no eye has seen, no ear has heard, what amazing things God has planned for those who love Him.'* Do we really believe that, that it's a Biblical truth? If that is the truth, then how do we get hold of that? How do we get to hear about it? Well, we start to ask God. We start to ask Him to be part of our thinking and our dreaming, so that we're not thinking small, but thinking big. We are dissolving the parameters.

For example: if we want enough money to pay our bills, then that's actually small-minded, orphan thinking. You may not think it is, you may think *'Oh gosh, I've never trusted God to pay my bills before, so this is a big step for me.'*

Indeed, it's a step in the right direction, but it's not the destination. I want enough money that I can *bless others* as well as paying my bills; I want there to be an overflow, so that I am actually able to give away almost more than what comes in. That's Kingdom perspective, and that kind of thinking generally attracts God's heart.

This can start happening in our lives if our focus is not on how much we have in our purse or wallet, but *on who God is,* and we're laying our needs at God's feet and we're starting to act in faith on those things.

I believe that we grow in these things. So our step in the right direction is a stretch – then when it is not, we're ready for more stretching. Each time we grow in something, we will need to step outside our comfort zone a bit.

Orphan mindsets make the focus about us, and if the focus is on us, then we're going to have a small dream. If we can give ourselves to God and turn the focus instead to what God wants, then we're releasing it to be a bigger picture.

When we're living for ourselves, the enemy has already stolen from us: he's stolen our destiny. We're *never* meant to live for ourselves, and when we live for God, the sky is not the limit, the universe is.

I've already talked about not being self-conscious, but where we're struggling with our issues, we can just be sin-conscious instead, which is a little step in the right direction, because godly sorrow is the start of repentance. However, the enemy wants us to be over-conscious of our sin, so we remain in his domain. It's only when, like I said earlier, we give things to God and focus on His love and His forgiveness, that sin-consciousness begins to lose its hold and we become more Who We Are In Christ.

As we become less sin-conscious, we become more *God-conscious,* more love-conscious. For some of us, our personalities and our spirits have grown in different ways, so that we're slightly deformed. So it may be that we're 'other-people-conscious', and that's great, but God didn't ask us to be 'other-people-conscious' first.

He asked us to be God-conscious first. He said 'love me with all your heart, mind, soul and strength.' Be God-conscious first (not religious, but God-conscious), because then we are propelled by love. When we're just other-people-conscious, then we're not necessarily propelled by love. You think you might be, but actually the kind of love you're giving other people is still lacking in God's eyes, because if He was first, the kind of love you would be giving other people would be even better. I've met people who love others, but don't love themselves. Well, that's breaking the 2nd commandment, as mentioned earlier. Jesus said to love others as we love ourselves, and I think that there's a play on words there. I think the 'as' is also about the process of loving other people from the Overflow of loving ourselves. That's an interpretation that I felt the Holy Spirit showed me one day. The important thing is not to be just other-people-focussed, and not to be self-focussed or sin-focussed, but to be God-focussed. Then we'll be dreaming with God, no doubt about it.

Interdependency Rules

God's dream for you is not *just for you*, it never was. God doesn't do *anything* just singular, He Himself lives interdependent: Father, Son and Holy Spirit. And so, if we're made in His image, male and female, that means that there are male and female attributes of God. Interdependency is how God is going to fulfil His plans for you. Sometimes the world's way of thinking is *'we want to do it by ourselves,'* but actually, it will never be the best it can be by ourselves. It's not the plan to, because part of the process of becoming who God's called us to be is the transforming aspect.

In order for us not to be self-focussed, and to be open and interdependent, God will use other people. He will use other people to fulfil his plans for you, and you need to be open to that, you need to welcome it.

We're never meant to be alone, and when Jesus left His disciples, He said *'I will be with you always and the Holy Spirit will lead you into truth.'* And so, God recognises that we're our best when we're not alone. There are varying degrees of isolation – not everyone likes to be in a crowd all the time – but it's important that we learn to work with people. I remember, years ago, being advised not to work in a team ministry, because there would be 'more pressures' and they 'never work well'. But you know, team is about people, and if I'm choosing to work with people, then I want those rough edges that are in my life to be rubbed off, and I want theirs to be rubbed off too.

Part of interdependency is God allowing us all to become more holy and more like Him. We need to be totally willing for Him to do it in His way, and He always uses other people to encourage, strengthen and direct. When we are working alone, the enemy has stolen from us, as we are working against what God made us for, and we are not living life in fullness.

Taking Back Our Dreams and Making Them a Reality

Many of us are dreamers. I know Martin Luther King had a dream, but I personally think that it was more of a vision, because lots of people dream and have inspired ideas, but do nothing about them.

In my mind, the difference between a dream and a vision is clear: people who have a dream just dream, and somehow expect their wishes and dreams to be fulfilled one day, out of nowhere.

Those who have a vision make it a reality through action; once they have the dream, they start to create steps to move from where they are, to where their vision is, usually with help from God-given passion, guidance, and Spirit-led opportunities (if we can recognise them!) along the way. I'll be talking more about this in another chapter.

So, I think Martin Luther King didn't just have a dream, he had a vision. And if we're going to take back our time and the priorities God has put on our lives, then we need to recognise we have a destiny, and our dreams are part of this, so we can start acting on them as God leads. We need to recognise that our little dream is part of who God created us to be, the song we were given to sing, as it were, and immensely important to God's overall plan.

Let's not lose sight of the fact that God calls us to live in intimacy with Him so that we experience the fullness in Him that Jesus spoke about. Our living in Overflow will affect every relationship we've got and every situation that we come across, and the wonderful thing is, nothing is a responsibility or burden, because Kingdom then just naturally happens. The Overflow does all the work, as we take hold of Who We Are In Christ and we fulfil our destiny.

We recognise our destiny by observing godly passions bubbling up in us. The Bible says:

> *Delight yourself also in the LORD, And He shall give you the desires of your heart.* (Psalm 37:4 NKJV)

Where we have a delightful intimacy with the Lord, then the Holy Spirit and our spirit, together, births or sharpens God-given dreams. (When we are born again, the Holy Spirit becomes permanently downloaded into us, and a new creation is born in us where godly passions and desires are kept that are part of who we are and what we are called to be.) If we don't step into our destiny, then the enemy is already stealing from us, from our families, from our friends.

Releasing the Flow

I often say to Jasper that he's '*not the man of my dreams!'* (with a cheeky smirk on my face). He knows that I tell everyone that he is *beyond* my wildest dreams, as is often the case when God gives us a gift.

God can give us what we need, but as I've already hinted, He doesn't give us *just* what we need.

In Philippians it says, *'My God will supply all your needs according to His riches in glory,'* (Philippians 4:19) which is immense, not just God supplying all my needs. And so, because His riches are immense, if there's one thing I see in testimonies of God, it's His greatness – how massive He is.

My mind is too small, my expectations are too limited, and the way God wants to bless me and others is *so much bigger than what I can conceive.* Get used to God blowing your mind!

If I come into my God-given destiny, then it doesn't just benefit me, it benefits you all as well. A friend, Sarah in our staff team, gets this well. I work as an unpaid minister and rely on God's provision through gifts. When I was recently given a gift, she was so delighted for me, as she knew that it was a sign that God's blessing would also overflow for her and others in our church family. We live having everything 'in common' and she gets it. I wish more people would!

If I won a million pounds, and we're family, I would be spending some of that money in a way that blesses you. Similarly, with spiritual gifts, if God blesses me with healing, freedom and laughter, then that isn't a blessing that will stay with myself, because God designed the spiritual world so that all blessing flows to others through its overflow. It's part of His nature.

'Just enough' is not Kingdom – look at all the accounts in the Bible. There's always abundance. Even in the feeding of the five thousand, there were baskets of food left over. You might think *'what a waste,'* but where there's only just enough, I don't believe that's Overflow – but constricted flow.

- We're on holiday in Seattle as a family at the moment, because God blew my mind. We gave our holiday away this year – but He gave us an even better one!

- I'm writing this book (much more easily) on an iPad, because a lady gave a gift to my ministry that blew my mind. It has made my writing so much easier.

- I'm married to a beautiful man because God blew my mind. My ministry is complemented because of his love and wisdom.

- I have a wonderful family who have already overcome many challenges because God blew my mind.

Get used to having your mind blown open and keep it open and un-constricted!

I used to find giving really hard, and that's because I had grown up in poverty, and I had a poverty mindset. I held onto the little I had very tightly, even to the extent that I would go for the biggest piece of cake, because my spirit was deprived, I felt that I deserved it. When we're living from that place, we're very much in the enemy's camp. Now, that may have been our experience, but if we want to see that change, then we need to become God-conscious in this area. Like I talked about lusts having a hold on us, this inability to give can also have a hold on us, and one of the things I recognised quite early in my Christian life is that *wherever I was reluctant to give, I needed to give more.* Initially, I never used to tithe, and I remember hearing a testimony about tithing when I was living in the States, in debt, and having food parcels from the church because we didn't have enough to make ends meet. I remember the conflict, because I knew it was important to tithe, but I also know that it was important to get rid of our credit card debt. And so, I said to God in my heart that I'd give 5% to my debt, and 5% to Him, and when I paid off my debt, that He would get the whole 10%. Not only was I able to give 10% within a year, but before 2 years was up, I was able to give Him 20% of my income! We went from a rented flat and no money to having a 4 bedroom, detached house and large income (on my husband's part) and no debt. And that Overflow started by giving.

God really does reward us for giving freely. When our capacity for giving is enlarged, so is our capacity for receiving.

When God called me to Sheffield, and also told me I'd have no debt when I moved, I thought I may have to sell my car, which was being paid off through a loan agreement. I kept my dilemma to myself and the Lord. A friend had suggested I get people to sponsor me when I moved, but when I read her letter I just knew that wasn't what God was calling me to. I told Him I would live by faith, but I wanted to live by *real* faith. Within a minute, my phone rang and a friend offered to pay off my car. I told her that I owed £5000 on it, but she still insisted. I was stunned, but God knew the decision I had just made to live off His grace, and He is a good father who loves to give good gifts! The girls and I did a little dance when the cheque arrived, delighting in His goodness.

I think part of what's behind first fruits and giving to God is keeping God-conscious about things and resources, so that we continue to look to Him, and not allow money to have a hold on us. And of course, offerings come on top of tithes, so I have to have a giving heart, and part of giving is about flow: as soon as I start to fear about my finances, and as soon as I start to act on that, the flow stops and the money dries up. Whenever I act in flow, God seems to provide. For example, this year we wanted to go on holiday, and we wanted to go on holiday but still bless other people. We decided to bless a family with a holiday, but it meant that it severely affected our ability to go on one ourselves. So I put a request in The Order Of Mission network (the family of churches which make them up) to see if anyone would be interested in doing a house swap, and it turns out that we went to Seattle! It was far beyond what I had expected, and it's just up God's street, because God always blesses me beyond my expectations, which says something about how small my mindset still is. I thought the timing was interesting in this story, because it was only after we gave away our holiday to someone else that God actually released the inspiration to enquire about a house swap. It's important that if we are giving, it's all about flow, and whenever something constricts flow, such as fear, we need to deal with the fear in order for the flow to progress.

It's important that we don't hold onto, or get too attached to anything in terms of things, or in terms of doing things a certain way, and it's important that we don't let attachments get re-attached. There are many occasions where I've given things to God, and 6 months later have found that they're still there, just like a cat that's found its way home; I need to put it outside again. I need to make sure that my boundaries are firmer, so that I don't allow my attachments to return. If I don't want to get attached to objects and things, then I will be careful where I put my mind. Some people struggle with pornography, so they need to completely avoid it, and they may need to avoid certain television programmes because they reawaken that attachment. Some people are attached to chocolate; I will not buy chocolate for the house. I made a decision not to buy it in, because if it's in, I'll eat it. It's a weakness, so a boundary has to come in place if I've made a decision about an attachment, to keep the attachments out. I want to be free to be moulded by God, and when I'm told to do something by God, not have an agenda already in place, but trust Him. I told you that I'm asking the Lord about my daily diet at the moment, and I'd got something in mind to eat that I fancied the other day, but I don't want this attachment, so I had to pray longer than I usually did, in order to not go for what I craved. Anything that has a hold on us isn't from God. If we want to Take Back What's Been Stolen, then we need to recognise where the attachments are. We need to dream big and to start to own Who We Are In Christ, in order to reawaken what God has created us to be.

So, if we are living from a place of Overflow, the biggest thing we are taking back from the enemy is... our destined lives. We're taking back how we spend our time, our gifts, who we are, our destiny. What better black-eye to give the enemy, than becoming all that God's called us to be?

> *Yes, you will be enriched in every way so that you can always be generous. And when we take your gifts to those who need them, they will thank God. So two good things will result from this ministry of giving – the needs of the believers in Jerusalem will be met, and they will joyfully express their thanks to God.*
> (2 Corinthians 9:11b-12 NKJV)

> *Give, and it will be given to you: good measure, pressed down, shaken together, and running over will be put into your bosom. For with the same measure that you use, it will be measured back to you.*
> (Luke 6:38 NKJV)

Are you being transformed to live in the wide expanse of all God wants to give you, or are you 'making do' with a limited lifestyle?

Life in Fullness

CHAPTER 8

Living from a Heavenly Place

A clergy friend of mine had some difficult experiences growing up which she kindly said I could share:

As a child, I used to get locked in a dark room and it distressed me greatly. It made me fearful and isolated. Years later, when I was training for ministry, a visiting speaker gave a Word of Knowledge about me locked in this room – and I wailed my eyes out. As he prayed for me, I saw myself back in that room again, and sensed him pulling my hand, as if he was pulling me out of the room. The next day, when I had a picnic with my pre-school daughter, we parked in a gateway. After she ate, she asked if she could get out of the car and go into the field. As she did so, she ran with delight into the field and sunshine and suddenly checked herself to see if it was OK to run off a bit, and turned around to seek my approval – I smiled and waved her on, so she turned round again and danced off into the field.

Suddenly, this picture was superimposed upon the memory of my being locked in a room – and it was no longer my young daughter springing with joy across the field, but me, who was suddenly released from darkness to bounce and enjoy the sunshine!

When we're healed by God, He re-writes history for us with an awesome and redemptive slant. The pain of our hurts keeps us earthed and focussed on earthly pain and justice, but as we're healed, it raises our gaze heavenward and frees and enables us to be enables us to be heaven– and eternally–focussed, not earthly– and temporary–focussed.

At the beginning of Colossians 3, we're encouraged to fix our minds on things that are above, where Christ is seated, because when we're born again, we enter a new reality and need to remain focussed on it:

> *If then you have been raised with Christ (to a new life, thus sharing His resurrection from the dead), aim at and seek the (rich, eternal treasures) that are above, where Christ is, seated at the right hand of God. And* ***set your minds and keep them set on what is above*** *(the higher things), not on the things that are on the earth. For (as far as this world is concerned)* ***you have died, and your (new, real) life is hidden with Christ in God.*** *When Christ, Who is our life, appears, then you also will appear with Him in (the splendour of His) glory.* (Colossians 3:1-3 Amplified)

When we re-fix our focus in this way, then our new reality becomes real for us. According to Paul in Colossians, we're no longer anchored to things that are on the earth: we have become part of God's eternal family. If we're just anchored to the earth, then we're going to be like a ship trying to sail whilst still anchored; we won't be able to travel.

To become completely God-destined, whatever our past, our focus must change from being earth-bound to heaven-ward.

Up to this point, we may have been preoccupied with earthly priorities: family, work, ministry, etc., but if we recognise that our real spiritual lives are hidden yet raised with Christ (resurrected to the victory of a son), then we'll carry a power and authority that comes from being raised with Christ, with an objectivity and heavenly perspective that is part of our new inheritance. This heavenly perspective doesn't just affect eternal things, but affects our whole lives, so that our earthly bodies, relationships and work demonstrate fullness and anointing. We prosper: mind, body and spirit.

Beloved, I pray that you may prosper in all things and be in health, just as your soul prospers. For I rejoiced greatly when brethren came and testified of the truth that is in you, just as you walk in the truth. (3 John 1:2 NKJV)

Living Heaven to Earth

If we're going to operate from a heavenly perspective, then we need to live there; we need to recognise that this is the place where we're rooted. We may still be operating *in* this world, but we're not supposed to be *of* this world.

In James, it says that a double-minded man is unstable in all his ways. I remember reading that a lot as a teenager, and I could never make my mind up. If I made a decision about something, I would always be second-guessing myself. Doubt would always be eating away at me. I was very double-minded, as the Bible would say. In order to keep the things that are precious to God from being robbed from us, we need to learn to become more anchored in God, more rooted in His love, more 'at one' with His acceptance.

If we're not accepting or forgiving *of* ourselves, then we can't do this. If we're putting another person's opinion above His opinion, then we can't do this. If we are overwhelmed by continuous doubts, then we can't do this. In order to be anchored, *we need to take what God says as final and not allow our internal dialogue and our rollercoaster feelings to affect the truth and stability of God's word.* If God says it, it's real. *'The steadfast love of the Lord never ceases.'* It's Biblical. So, His love for me is steadfast, it's not up and down, it doesn't change with His mood. His mercies never come to an end, His truth is Biblical. If I need mercy, there's only one place where I am going to find it forever – in God's hands. His mercies are new every morning, how amazing is that?

In other words, if I feel bad today because I messed up yesterday, I can come to God knowing that His mercies are new. He's not upset with me, He loves me and knows me, He knows the issues I struggle with are carnal, and that I'm knocked about by all the 'powers and principalities', as the Bible says. He also knows my heart for Him and my desires. So, I can always approach Him, because His mercies are always new every morning and they're steadfast. *I need to ensure that Biblical truth becomes rooted in me.*

Godly sorrow is what the Holy Spirit produces, not heavy guilt. If we're anchored in God, then we are not going to allow the lies of the enemy, the so-called wisdom of the world, or the unpredictability of our feelings to pull us out of that place of being rooted in Him and His love.

I went through a challenging two years, having got rid of various issues, and God asked me to meditate on Colossians 3 for a month. I couldn't understand why. But as a Christian leader, I had recognised bits of self-bitterness were still present from time to time and I was trying to deal with those, whilst at the same time dealing with a whole load of accusation, externally and internally. I was trying to keep the accuser out of my mind, but with different things that were going on in ministry and other things that kept coming against me, the enemy made sure that it was hard work.

Meditating on Colossians 3 helped me to recognise that my life was *abiding* in Christ; I didn't need to be preoccupied by earthly things – they just weren't important in comparison. My life in Him was. At about this time, we had a prayer meeting at church, and I woke that morning and a thought popped into my head: *'I want you to wear white.'* I knew it was God, but I didn't know why. I remember going downstairs to say to my husband *'Do you want the good news or the bad news? The good news is I've heard from God, the bad news is that He's told me He wants me to wear white and I don't have anything white in my wardrobe – can I have some money to go and buy some?'*

Now all the clothes in my wardrobe are white. I wasn't sure at the time what God was trying to do in asking me to wear white. Was it to exemplify that I am a new creation or the bride of Christ? Well, I wasn't sure, but I am pleased that I have a continual reminder as I wear white, that I have power over the enemy when I remember to stay seated and anchored in heavenly places. This is the place we naturally Overflow from, remember?

One day, just after I'd been on a Christian conference, my family and I went on holiday to visit relatives by the sea. We were looking round a museum when someone asked *'Is there a doctor here?'*

I said *'Well, I'm not a doctor, I'm a nurse, can I help?'*

There was a woman collapsed outside, so I went and had a look at her. It was an elderly woman, collapsed on a bench, with her husband shouting *'Come on Bertha!'* Now, her name wasn't Bertha, I just can't remember what it was, but for the purposes of this story we'll call her Bertha. Her husband just kept shouting *'Come on Bertha!'* and I suggested that he tell her how much she meant to him, because if it was me, and I was leaving this world, then I would want to hear something like that, not someone stressing out over me. I got quite irritated in my spirit with this guy, because he couldn't see that his wife was dying. At the time, I was a nursing matron and I prided myself on knowing when someone's time was up before it happened, so that I could appoint a nurse to sit with them as they died and make it as comforting for them as possible.

I examined Bertha and noticed that her femoral pulse had almost gone, her breathing was erratic, and while I stood there, taking her pulse, she just died; her pupils dilated, she stopped breathing, her pulse went, she was dead. There was a conflict in my mind: it was quite obvious that her husband wanted her back, but she was an old lady and I wasn't sure if cardiac massage would have any effect.

I was staring closely into her dilated pupils while I was having this thought, and all of a sudden I found myself praying in tongues under my breath; it was entirely unconscious and I'd only just started doing it. The moment I became conscious that I was speaking in tongues, Bertha's pupils popped back and she took a deep breath in. My face being so close to hers, I nearly bit my tongue in half – I was shocked! She started breathing again much to my and her husband's amazement. At about that time, the ambulance arrived and took her inside, and I sat with her husband on the bench for about 10 or 15 minutes, and when they emerged I asked if she had died. They said *'Oh no she's fine, we just put a drip in.'* I was just stunned.

I came away from that episode and asked God what happened, and the Holy Spirit rebuked me. He told me, *'It is not for you to say when someone's time is up'.*

I was ashamed and realised that I'd allowed my 'so-called' professionalism to get in the way of what God had wanted. I wasn't seated in a heavenly place at all! I was firmly rooted in an earthly place. God brought this woman back from the dead. I didn't. That's why when people ask if I've seen the dead raised I say yes, but I laugh when I recognise it had absolutely nothing to do with my faith and more to do with Living From The Overflow.

Now, however, in similar situations, I *always* ask God first and I have more faith to see the dead raised back to life than to see a common cold cured. We always need to be conscious of God and what He wants for our lives. We need to be conscious of Him in every decision we make.

You see, if we're not raised with Christ in our faith, firmly seated in heavenly places, then we're not going to ask those important questions – we're just going to be earthed. We don't want to be just earthed, as Christians, because we'll miss God's glory displayed (or Him 'showing off' as I sometimes say!) and we'll miss our inheritance. So it's really important that we have the right perspective.

Jesus said to His followers that they would *do even greater work* than He did, and He said '*everything is possible for those who believe.*' So really, *all you need* is belief.

> *I tell you the truth, anyone who believes in me will do the same works I have done, and even greater works, because I am going to be with the Father.*
> (John 14:12 NLT)

Our belief here is not dependent on us, our goodness or greatness. It's dependant on the power of God, and if we can take our eyes off our issues and struggles, and place our trust in God and what He can do, then *with God, everything is possible* (Matthew 19:26 NKJV). Then we will Take Back What The Enemy Has Stolen from us.

Overcoming Fear with Faith

In 2 Chronicles 20, King Jehoshaphat was a bit freaked out, because the three nations that had bullied Israel (that God had said to avoid) were coming against him – all together. Jehoshaphat was *very* stressed.

Immediately he called a fast, turned to God and said *'we don't know what to do, but our eyes are on you.'* He did this publicly, in front of his people, so that they could see that he didn't know what to do, and to show them that he was focussing on God. He was leading by example. They all fasted and prayed, asking God for guidance. At that point, God spoke through a prophet, Metaniah, and he said:

> *Do not be afraid nor dismayed because of this great multitude,* **for the battle is not yours, but God's.** *Tomorrow go down against them. They will surely come up by the Ascent of Ziz, and you will find them at the end of the brook before the Wilderness of Jeruel.* **You will not need to fight in this battle. Position yourselves, stand still and see the salvation of the Lord, who is with you**, *O Judah and Jerusalem! Do not fear or be dismayed; tomorrow go out against them, for the Lord is with you.* (2 Chronicles 20:15b-17)

Jehoshaphat went to bed, and when he awoke the next morning he got everybody praying again. *They went to the place they were told to, and they praised God.* The Bible says that when they started to praise God, it confused the enemy. When we praise God, the enemy hates it; he can't stick his fingers in his ears deep enough! Praise drives him out, and you'll see a lot of people who will connect better with God by having a time of prayer and worship.

Praise and worship help us to refocus on *'the things that are above, not on earthly things.'* It helps us to express our love and trust in God and Psalm 22:3 (in the King James Version) says that *'God inhabits the praises of His people Israel'.* No wonder the enemy can't stand it!

If we're going to be operating from a heavenly place, we need to use our heavenly tools. Praise and intercession are fundamental to Taking Back What The Enemy Has Stolen. If

Jehoshaphat had allowed fear to come in instead, then the likelihood is that their focus would not have been on God; they would have fear ruling them and confusion would have been on their side, not that of the enemy. Instead, they had a clear head, and did exactly what God said; they didn't allow fear to come in, and they sent the enemy packing.

> *There is no fear in love; but perfect love casts out fear, because fear involves torment. But he who fears has not been made perfect in love.* (1 John 4:8 NKJV)

Fear is one of the things which plagues the Church, and Jesus wants to see us released from it.

Fear is probably the biggest stumbling block in the Christian life. I think that it's one of the enemy's biggest tools. It's important we deal with fear, and it's one of those things that we should deal with sooner rather than later. I thought I had dealt with fear for many years, but actually I had just learnt to *manage* my fear. I wanted to kick out my fear. I went on a conference a few years ago, and realised that I had kicked out many of the things they were talking about, but the one thing I hadn't kicked out was fear. I did this at that conference, and I've not let it back in since. Fear and I have had the odd scuffle every now and again, when it wants to come back in my life, but God's had the upper hand.

> *The LORD is my light and my salvation; whom shall I fear?* ***The LORD is the strength of my life; of whom shall I be afraid?*** (Psalm 27:1 NKJV)

> *In God I have put my trust; I will not fear. What can flesh do to me?* (Psalm 56:3-5 NKJV)

So, we need to deal with things like fear; fear causes us not just to think small, but to focus on the problem and not see God at all. I had fear as a filter, and I can tell you that it does an enormous amount to change your perspective.

Now that I don't have it, I see every situation differently – it's the same when we get rid of any stronghold, we see differently. But fear is one of the major things which will prevent us from receiving all God wants to give us, so the sooner we kick it out, the better.

I used to think I was the most organised person on earth, but I just had fear. I just thought that I was like a girl guide, but actually it was fear that was driving me. Fear just helped me to imagine the worst case scenario all the time. It controlled me and made me pressure others, because of my insecurities.

Also, I had fear of man. In other words, I was worried about what people thought of me, and how well they accepted me dictated how well I thought of myself. Silly, I know, but I know many who do this. I think King Saul in the Old Testament also had this problem. If we have fear of man (and are people-pleasers), then we will prioritise others or the enemy's agenda above God's. Such fear leaves us restless, we will not have peace and the decisions we make will not be Spirit-inspired.

It's very hard to hear the Holy Spirit at all when we're fearing; in fact it's almost impossible to hear Him clearly. Wisdom will have little effect, because we are, in essence, listening to the enemy when we are listening to fear.

If I recognise that I'm getting stressed, I know I'm putting myself in a place where I'm not going to be able to hear God very clearly, so the first thing that I want to do is put my mind at peace so I can hear and think clearly. So I position myself to strengthen my spirit in the Lord. This is why in Philippians 4:6 it says '*do not worry about anything, but pray about everything.*'

In other words, when anxiety comes knocking, I use it as a signal to pray about whatever is troubling me.

When you give your worry to God in a prayer, you're actually getting rid of fear in that area. When you plant a truth where that particular fear used to be, then you keep it out of there for good.

> *Don't worry about anything; instead, pray about everything. Tell God what you need, and thank him for all he has done. Then you will experience God's peace, which exceeds anything we can understand. His peace will guard your hearts and minds as you live in Christ Jesus.*
> (Philippians 4:6-7 NLT)

I'm pretty good, now, at giving my concerns to God, which means I can live from a place of peace. In exchange for my fear, I have planted biblical truths which have deepened my trust in God to provide my every need, and have helped me see that God loves me unconditionally. I only want to live to please Him, not others, so I need not worry about what others think of me.

Having given our concerns to God (kicked out fear), we experience God's peace, which brings a renewed perspective. This is the place we want to live in. But look what else comes as part of the package:

> *For God has not given us a spirit of fear, but of* ***power*** *and of* ***love*** *and of a* ***sound mind****.* (2 Timothy 1:7 NKJV)

Power, love and a sound mind are wonderful rewards for overcoming fear, and are all much needed in the Church today. I often pray for the Church, that it overcomes fear in every respect.

The Freedom of Forgiveness

> *But when you are praying, first forgive anyone you are holding a grudge against, so that your Father in heaven will forgive your sins, too.* (Mark 11:25 NLT)

> *Be angry, and do not sin: do not let the sun go down on your wrath.* (Ephesians 4:25-27 NKJV)

Another stronghold that Jesus emphasised which needs to be completely eradicated is Unforgiveness, also known as bitterness.

I don't want to repeat a lot about this, as it is a large subject and if you wish to know more, see my book *Hurt Without Hate: The Transforming Power Of Forgiveness.*

Bitterness (vengeance, anger, hate, etc.) brings division, and is the very opposite of what Jesus came to bring, which is unity based in love.

> *Love prospers when a fault is forgiven, but dwelling on it separates close friends.* (Proverbs 17:9 NLT)

Can we learn to forgive like God does? We may think we have forgiven, but if we keep remembering someone's sin, then we haven't forgiven like God has. You see, God *forgets* our sins as part of forgiving us. Isn't that amazing? God wants us to know He forgets our sin. The enemy doesn't *ever* want us to forget our sin.

Obviously, heinous sin needs strict consequences, and strict boundaries to prevent recurrence, but most of our sin doesn't fall into this category.

You may say, *'I don't want to forget another's sin because they may hurt me again.'* Well, we learn, don't we, to create boundaries to protect that which is precious in ourselves and others, and we can *still* do that *whilst* forgiving. I can forgive a bully, but I will not make the same mistake twice. I can forgive, but trust must be earned.

However, if we continue to remember someone's sin, without giving opportunities for change, then we will never be able to move on emotionally, or allow them to be viewed differently in our eyes. We may feel led to be judging towards them, but Jesus said we must not judge, but honour each other, which means we need to not just have short accounts, but almost no accounts of their sin!

Setting the record straight sets the gauge at zero and the opportunity for moving forward is created. Just like we love because He first loved us, we forgive because He first forgave us. Who are we to withhold forgiveness to anyone, when we expect *our* sins forgiven?

In the following story, the unforgiving servant does not allow the grace and mercy shown to him to flow *through* him to others, because he would not forgive (and forget) in the same way that forgiveness had been demonstrated to him:

> *Then Peter came to him and asked, "Lord, how often should I forgive someone who sins against me? Seven times?" "No, not seven times," Jesus replied, "but seventy times seven! Therefore, the Kingdom of Heaven can be compared to a king who decided to bring his accounts up to date with servants who had borrowed money from him. In the process, one of his debtors was brought in who owed him millions of dollars. He couldn't pay, so his master ordered that he be sold – along with his wife, his children, and everything he owned – to pay the debt.*

"But the man fell down before his master and begged him, 'Please, be patient with me, and I will pay it all.' Then his master was filled with pity for him, and he released him and forgave his debt. But when the man left the king, he went to a fellow servant who owed him a few thousand dollars. He grabbed him by the throat and demanded instant payment. His fellow servant fell down before him and begged for a little more time. 'Be patient with me, and I will pay it,' he pleaded. But his creditor wouldn't wait. He had the man arrested and put in prison until the debt could be paid in full.

"When some of the other servants saw this, they were very upset. They went to the king and told him everything that had happened. Then the king called in the man he had forgiven and said, 'You evil servant! I forgave you that tremendous debt because you pleaded with me. Shouldn't you have mercy on your fellow servant, just as I had mercy on you?' Then the angry king sent the man to prison to be tortured until he had paid his entire debt.

"That's what my heavenly Father will do to you if you refuse to forgive your brothers and sisters from your heart." (Matthew 18:21-35 NLT)

When we are fixing our minds on those things which are above and seated in heavenly places, not only do we hear the love of the Father with clarity and intimacy, but we will have heaven's perspective and be able to Take Back What The Enemy Has Stolen with power! Remember Bertha!

Living from a heavenly place

CHAPTER 9

Woven Together

Alone we can do so little; together we can do so much. (Helen Keller)

Love Acts

God loves unity. The enemy *hates* unity. God loves us. The enemy *hates* us! We're the object of the Father's affection. That means the enemy *hates us even more*. God loves us each individually and He adores us as His Church. The enemy hates us individually and corporately as a Church, the Body of Christ.

Jesus said that there would be something unique about Jesus' followers (among the many groups around): that everyone would see and take note of the nature of our love for each other.

> *A new commandment I give to you, that* ***you love one another; as I have loved you****, that you also love one another.* ***By this all will know that you are My disciples,*** *if you have love for one another.* (John 13:34-35 NKJV)

This quote isn't just superficial love, or love that is expressed with lots of words. It's love that is demonstrated by sacrificial action – laying down one's life.

We're not called to lay down our lives for another person's agenda (because the enemy can control us through other people's expectations and we're to live to God's agenda). But we are called to express His love for others through action (only easy-yoke and Spirit-led, living from Overflow). You see, to help others come to know of God's love, sometimes people need to see and receive a radical expression of love as the Spirit leads.

> *Suppose you see a brother or sister who has no food or clothing, and you say, "Good-bye and have a good day; stay warm and eat well"—but then you don't give that person any food or clothing. What good does that do? So you see,* ***faith by itself isn't enough. Unless it produces good deeds, it is dead and useless.***
>
> *Now someone may argue, "Some people have faith; others have good deeds." But I say, "How can you show me your faith if you don't have good deeds? I will show you my faith by my good deeds."* (James 2:14b-18 NLT)

Interdependency Grows and Supports

There's an intimacy of love in relationships which we are all created for. Whether or not your experience of being alongside others has been good or bad; whether or not we're an introvert or extrovert; whether or not we even *like* people, we are created to be in community and be interdependent.

In Acts 2 we see real community, 'Oikos' (which is the Greek word for extended family). The interdependence the disciples model demonstrates that not only are they reliant on each other to be conduits of God's provision, guidance and support, but they feel a loving responsibility towards each other.

> *Now all who believed were together, and had all things in common, and sold their possessions and goods, and divided them among all, as anyone had need. So continuing daily with one accord in the temple, and breaking bread from house to house, they ate their food with gladness and simplicity of heart.* (Acts 2:44-46 NKJV)

This kind of community is how God sees family. A bit like the God-head – same vision, particular roles and passions, varied in nature with a high interdependence.

As people, we have a greater tendency to collaborate *when it's in our best interest,* because we are often self-focussed. When it's 'worth our while'. Independence has been a fashionable word in recent years and implies an objectivity and detachment. However, in relationships, independence demonstrates inward-looking, self-focussed thinking which can lead to building our own empire, instead of modelling our lives on God's Kingdom.

Where there is a lack of openness to others, there is often no collaboration or genuine appreciation for another's contribution. Often, fear or pride can be involved. We can be fearful of getting hurt or pressured, of our vision (*our* 'baby'), being taken away from us. Where we no longer have these faulty thoughts, we can have a deeper appreciation for one another's gifts and contributions, and genuinely see the many advantages of being interdependent. Once there are healthy boundaries in place, an agreement over expectations, and a clear vision expressed and committed to, then interdependence can be a wonderful foundation for fullness.

Division Destroys

Division and strife will cause us to want to live independent of others, so that we do not feel rejected, pressured, controlled, frustrated, hurt, criticised, or made to feel bad about who we are. Many good, but fragile people have left churches because they expected the gentle accepting love of Christ to be the church atmosphere, and instead experienced the back-biting, critical and defensive behaviour that leaks out of the un-sanctified parts of us all.

This is why we are encouraged to rid ourselves of these things:

> *So I say, let the Holy Spirit guide your lives. Then you won't be doing what your sinful nature craves. The sinful nature wants to do evil, which is just the opposite of what the Spirit wants. And the Spirit gives us desires that are the opposite of what the sinful nature desires. These two forces are constantly fighting each other, so you are not free to carry out your good intentions. But when you are directed by the Spirit, you are not under obligation to the law of Moses.*
>
> *When you follow the desires of your sinful nature, the results are very clear: sexual immorality, impurity, lustful pleasures, idolatry, sorcery, hostility, quarrelling, jealousy, outbursts of anger, selfish ambition, dissension, division, envy, drunkenness, wild parties, and other sins like these. Let me tell you again, as I have before, that anyone living that sort of life will not inherit the Kingdom of God.*
> (Galatians 5:16-21 NLT)

There's a harmony and 'One-ness' in heaven. The Father sees us as woven together; the Kingdom always emulates interdependency.

Forgiveness Integrates

Independence from God came to Adam and Eve when they decided to follow their own wisdom and not God's. Their independence from each other came when blame entered their relationship. Blame is part of the accuser's way of functioning and leads to accusation and bitterness.

Families have disagreements, and *living a Christ-life isn't having no disagreements, but learning to exercise forgiveness* so that we become more like God.

Jesus talks again and again about forgiveness; our ability to forgive ourselves, God, and each other is so fundamental to the Kingdom that Jesus says *we can't be in the Kingdom if we can't forgive.* I mean, how clear can you be?

> *If we confess our sins, He is faithful and just to forgive us our sins and to cleanse us from all unrighteousness.*
> (1 John 1:9 NKJV)

If we're going to have a forgiving heart, then we need to learn to separate the sin from the sinner and recognise that while something may feel personal, its personal feel comes from the enemy, not necessarily from the person. It's a spiritual battle we are in, remember; not a people one.

'Love is patient, love is kind' says 1 Corinthians 13; the primary driving force in all our relationships should be love. Where there's love, there's a woven-togetherness that the Bible describes as 'Koinonia' (Greek word). This passage describes 'Koinonia' perfectly.

> *Behold, how good and how pleasant it is for brethren to dwell together in unity!*
>
> *It is like the precious oil upon the head, running down on the beard,*
>
> *The beard of Aaron, running down on the edge of his garments.*
>
> *It is like the dew of Hermon, descending upon the mountains of Zion;*
>
> *For there the Lord commanded the blessing –*
> *Life forevermore.* (Psalm 133:1-3 NKJV)

Community Covers

In spiritual warfare, we are called to stand firm, fully equipped with our armour, but it's a corporate armour, as well as an individual one. You can't operate a roman shield properly and effectively without everyone working together, because only your front is protected when you try and use it by yourself. We need someone to cover our heads and backs – that is what we are supposed to do for each other. It's really important that we understand God's heart when it comes to being woven together. We are all adopted into the one family through God as our Father and there are expectations that, as a family, we will work together and operate as one. This applies in every respect of living: caring, sharing, encouraging, enabling and releasing.

Humility Creates Honour

There's a synergy that happens when we operate together. I can lift some things as one person, but I can lift more than twice as much with two people. So when we're feeling offended because someone's hurt us, or feeling isolated or rejected, etc., we need to deal with those things sooner rather than later; we need to spend time with God, and try and do as Jesus outlined in Matthew 18: talk with those we've fallen out with and make our relationships right.

There are key issues that are part of the process of Matthew 18, however, that I believe many in the church miss (I did!) and which are part of doing Matthew 18 effectively. The next few verses outline a key point which I believe Jesus makes as He shares stories leading up to the well known passage in Matthew 18 about how to resolve conflict:

> *Therefore whoever* ***humbles himself*** *as this little child is the greatest in the kingdom of heaven.* (Matthew 18:4 NKJV)

I was a listening to a friend of mine the other day, Gareth Davies, say that to pray *'Lord, teach me humility'* was entirely unbiblical – and he's right! The Bible says we are to *humble ourselves* – not ask Him to do it for us!

> *Likewise you younger people, submit yourselves to your elders. Yes, all of you be submissive to one another, and be clothed with humility, for*
>
> *"God resists the proud but gives grace to the humble."*
>
> *Therefore humble yourselves under the mighty hand of God, that He may exalt you in due time, casting all your care upon Him, for He cares for you.*
>
> (1 Peter 5:5-7 NKJV)

When we humble ourselves, the Lord hears us:

> *Then he said to me, "Do not fear, Daniel, for* ***from the first day that you set your heart to understand, and to humble yourself before your God, your words were heard;*** *and I have come because of your words".*
>
> (Daniel 10:12 NKJV)
>
> *Woe to the world because of offences! For offences must come, but woe to that man by whom the offence comes!*
>
> (Matthew 18:7 NKJV)

So when we fall out with (or offend) someone, knowing that we may have a fault or weakness should humble us, as we approach that person to have a 'Matthew 18' meeting. If we refuse to resolve conflict and by so doing, cause another person to sin, then Jesus says here that we're in big trouble! It sounds like Jesus is suggesting that we need to listen to, and examine, our own hearts; to accept responsibility for our own weaknesses before having our meeting.

"Take heed that you do not despise one of these little ones, for I say to you that in heaven their angels always see the face of My Father who is in heaven. For the Son of Man has come to save that which was lost.

"What do you think? If a man has a hundred sheep, and one of them goes astray, does he not leave the ninety-nine and go to the mountains to seek the one that is straying? And if he should find it, assuredly, I say to you, he rejoices more over that sheep than over the ninety-nine that did not go astray. Even so it is not the will of your Father who is in heaven that one of these little ones should perish." (Matthew 18:19-14 NKJV)

Our hearts need to be right as we come to resolve a conflict. There is no mention here of blame or right or wrong, but *of delight over someone lost being saved. We're told to speak the truth with love* – I do not encourage anyone to speak truth to anyone if they can't say it in love (Ephesians 4:15), or else we would indeed bruise one another.

The Bible says that if your brother sins against you, then you're not to leave it, but go and tell him – but tell him in love, so that he is most honoured. Don't talk about it to other people out of martyrdom or superiority, because that's the very competitiveness that Jesus wants to get rid of – it comes from the enemy. If your brother has heard you and you 'make up', then you have woven your relationship closer; if he doesn't hear you, then you can then say that you have been honest and clear with him, and you can choose whether or not to invest in your relationship.

Repay no one evil for evil. Have regard for good things in the sight of all men. If it is possible, as much as depends on you, live peaceably with all men. Beloved, do not avenge yourselves, but rather give place to wrath; for it is written, "Vengeance is Mine, I will repay," says the Lord. (Romans 12:17-19 NKJV)

Jesus goes on to talk about the parable of the unforgiving servant. Forgiveness is the main thing we need to understand about being woven together. If we can learn to forgive, then any relationship is easy, but it takes time to learn how to forgive. Don't let anything get in the way of relationships. That doesn't mean that you're always going to be at peace with all people, but *as far as it concerns you*, be at peace with all people.

So, honouring the person and humbling ourselves as we approach conflict with another is what Matthew 18 is really all about. It helps accountability, and you know we'll automatically have a spiritual covering, because we're acting God's way. We need to be aware that the enemy will use the weaknesses of people close to you to discourage you – that's what we call friendly fire – but we're to keep on forgiving.

We need to have a fear of God about each other. The Bible says *'do not touch the Lord's anointed.'* If the Lord has anointed someone for something, and you bad-mouth them or come against them in some way, then you're walking into the enemy's territory. That is not what God wants. Everyone has their faults, but if we help each other, are godly advocates to each other, and share what we see in love, it should restore them. But if we slander and gossip about someone, or are just downright rude to people that God loves and anoints, then we are walking into a minefield, because the Lord will withdraw a hand of blessing where we're bad-mouthing someone God loves immensely.

Being woven together is part of what the Holy Spirit is doing. I would encourage you not to let the enemy throw anything in your path that would stop you loving and honouring.

Love for the Enemy

The love for equals is a human thing – of friend for friend, brother for brother. It is to love what is loving and lovely. The world smiles.

The love for the less fortunate is a beautiful thing – the love for those who suffer, for those who are poor, the sick, the failures, the unlovely. This is compassion, and it touches the heart of the world.

The love for the more fortunate is a rare thing – to love those who succeed where we fail, to rejoice without envy with those who rejoice, the love of the poor for the rich, of the black man for the white man. The world is always bewildered by its saints.

And then there is the love for the enemy – love for the one who does not love you but mocks, threatens, and inflicts pain. The tortured's love for the torturer. This is God's love. It conquers the world. (Author unknown)

CHAPTER 10

Know Your Rights

Who I Am In My Authority

There is a lot I could say on this subject. However, at this point, I am going to list a few things which may not be covered elsewhere which I hope will help you to Take Back What The Enemy Has Stolen.

What saddens me is that as Christians, we don't know our rights, and because we don't know our spiritual legal rights, we don't enforce them. We get robbed and we don't do anything about it and then the enemy has defeated us in the area of our fullness and won, to a certain extent.

I say I'm saddened by this, but to be fair, I've actually lived most of my life in that place, and the reason I'm sad is because I've allowed the enemy to steal so much from me by my lack of awareness. He's stolen my time, my imagination, my creativity, and all kinds of things from my identity, all because I didn't know Who I Was and Am In Christ.

Our Rights Count

As a British Citizen, I have certain rights, at home and abroad. If I was abroad and facing trouble, I could turn to the British Embassy for help. Similarly, as a Christian, and because I'm in God, I have rights that are part and parcel of Who I Am in Christ. They are part of my inheritance, because of who my heavenly Father is; the resources and parameters He has set for me as one of His own.

Our ignorance doesn't help because the enemy is a deceiver and a liar. He's a sneaky little 'so-and-so' and he *doesn't* play fair. He *knows* where we don't know our authority better than we do, because *where we don't know our authority, he will already have free reign.* So the sooner we get informed, the better.

I recently heard of someone whose neighbour had taken more of their garden than they should have for a building extension, and the person affected said *'there's nothing I can do about it now.'* I *knew* that, actually, they *could* do something: they could contact the council and say that there hadn't been permission, and being against the law, they could have had that thing taken down. They either didn't know their authority, or were choosing not to use it because they didn't want the consequences.

Don't allow the enemy to intimidate you into doing nothing. Like when I may speed when no one's looking, but slow down for speed cameras, similarly, the enemy will try and get away with what he can, and only go on his way when he is sent.

The Enemy Interferes with Our Intimacy with God

I'm not trying to teach you how to be intimate with God in this short section, but simply want to explain some major factors which prevent intimacy.

Unbelief, independence, bitterness towards God, rebellion and a controlling spirit will all stifle intimacy with God; but as soon as we turn away from these things, we can run into the arms of our Father like the prodigal son returning home. I used to overspill with frustration and bitterness, and turned to self-bitterness whenever I tried to rebuke the enemy and consequently, it didn't work. God allowed that to continue *until* I died to frustration and bitterness. God does not tempt us, but *will allow difficulties* to test our hearts, minds and spirits so that we can quickly start living according to God's truth.

> *... No temptation has overtaken you except such as is common to man; but God is faithful, who will not allow you to be tempted beyond what you are able, but with the temptation will also make the way of escape, that you may be able to bear it.* (1 Corinthians 10:13 NKJV)
>
> *Trust in the Lord, and do good; Dwell in the land, and feed on His faithfulness. Delight yourself also in the Lord, and He shall give you the desires of your heart. Commit your way to the Lord, Trust also in Him, And He shall bring it to pass.*
>
> *He shall bring forth your righteousness as the light, and your justice as the noonday. Rest in the Lord, and wait patiently for Him; Do not fret because of him who prospers in his way, Because of the man who brings wicked schemes to pass. Cease from anger, and forsake wrath; Do not fret – it only causes harm.* (Psalm 37:3-8 NKJV)

Spiritual Gifts Empower Us Against the Enemy

The spiritual gifts outlined in the Bible are not given for any other reason than for the Body of Christ to be able to hear God's voice clearly, and empower us to do His will on earth.

> *Now concerning spiritual gifts, brethren, I do not want you to be ignorant: You know that you were Gentiles, carried away to these dumb idols, however you were led. Therefore I make known to you that no one speaking by the Spirit of God calls Jesus accursed, and*

> *no one can say that Jesus is Lord except by the Holy Spirit. There are diversities of gifts, but the same Spirit. There are differences of ministries, but the same Lord. And there are diversities of activities, but it is the same God who works all in all. But* **the manifestation of the Spirit is given to each one for the profit of all***: for to one is given the* **word of wisdom** *through the Spirit, to another the* **word of knowledge** *through the same Spirit, to another* **faith** *by the same Spirit, to another* **gifts of healings** *by the same Spirit, to another the* **working of miracles***, to another* **prophecy,** *to another* **discerning of spirits***, to another* **different kinds of tongues,** *to another* **the interpretation of tongues.** *But one and the same Spirit works all these things, distributing to each one individually as He wills.* (1 Corinthians 12:1-11 NKJV)

Nurture spiritual gifts not for what they are, but for what they can do in the hands of our Saviour.

There's a habit in the Church where people pray *'Enemy, I tell you to go in the name of Jesus,'* and they say *'and now come Holy Spirit'*, without waiting to see whether or not the enemy has gone!

We have been given spiritual gifts of prophecy and discernment to help us overcome the enemy, and we need to exercise these in prayer ministry. I remember when we had a really good church weekend with a visiting speaker and just as it started, one of the leader's sons was ill. He had just suddenly started feeling sick. I went and prayed, and as we were praying I saw something that looked like his spirit had something wrapped around it; a bit like a pole with a scarf or a snake wrapped around it. I felt the illness was the enemy, and that he was trying to get attached, so we rebuked the sickness and told it to go, but it stayed. My friend started to say *'Thank you Lord, come Holy Spirit,'* but I could still see in my mind that this thing was still wrapped around him. So I said *'hang on a minute, he (the enemy) has not gone, let's just pray in tongues for a bit,'* and I said to the enemy *'I can see that you are still there, and I'm telling you that you need to go now in the name of Jesus.'* I enforced my rights over that sickness, and as we prayed in tongues and I enforced my rights, it loosened and it went. The enemy is shocked when we can see him. I would encourage you to use the spiritual gifts, both for yourself and with others when you're beginning to take back this territory, because you may get the techniques right, but the enemy knows when you can't see him. So ask the Holy Spirit to give a revelation to you, so that you can kick the enemy out!

Healthy Coveting

To help us in delivering someone, we can covet the gifts we need to help us.

> *But* ***earnestly desire*** *the best gifts...*
> (1 Corinthians 12:31 NKJV)

> *Therefore, brethren,* ***desire earnestly*** *to prophesy, and do not forbid to speak with tongues.*
> (1 Corinthians 14:39 NKJV)

We're allowed to covet spiritual things if our motives and heart are right, but we cannot covet physical things. That's because we're to seek God first, and if a gift enables us to grow in intimacy with Him or bless others like He wishes, He cannot wait to give them to us. Anything else can take the place of God in our lives which is why He tells us not to covet anything which could become an idol.

You may not have a certain gift that you need, but do not worry. You have the Holy Spirit in you! He is the giver of all these gifts, and He can give you any one of these gifts at any time as you have need – remember Bertha!

Where God Guides, He Provides

We never need to worry about God supplying what we need as we step out (I know this is the third time I've mentioned God supplying our needs, but it's important!) if we are following the Spirit's lead. But there are times when we have not sought the leading of the Spirit, and may find ourselves in a pickle. We've all done this and I think God allows this so that we learn to walk closely with Him.

Whilst we're waiting for our answer, it is important to thank God for what He has already given before you see the end fruit: an attitude of gratitude needs to develop, and is key to seeing the whole harvest come in!

One day, recently, we found ourselves car-less. One car had died just before Christmas and the other was in an accident. We were wondering how we were going to pay for a new one and when I came home a friend of ours, Ruth, said that she was sharing a car with a friend who was happy to share it with us as well, as they lived locally.

It wasn't what we had planned or had even done before, and given our busy lives, I wasn't sure it would work. But God had us do that for a season and it worked well. Be open to Him answering you in ways you don't expect. There will always be a reason for it, and we learnt a lot during that period about *'having all things in common'* (Acts 2) and I'm grateful for it. My husband and I both have cars at the moment and I'm praying for one that is automatic, diesel and bigger than what I have. I know He will supply my need according to His riches, but He told me this week that I am to give my current car away before I get the one I'm praying for. He always keeps stretching us, because the same faith we use to trust Him for provision is the same faith we use to raise the dead!

Function Differs

We may have one purpose, but be used by God in different ways within that purpose.

David was anointed as King, but it was years before he actually became King. Meanwhile, he continued to do what God called him to do in the first place – honour and support His leader, King Saul. He could have taken Saul's kingdom forcibly, or even killed him in self-defence, but he chose to follow the Spirit's lead and allowed God to promote him to his calling in the right time.

We all have certain callings on our life, but we are to exercise them according to the Spirit's leading. Sometimes we are asked to take a step up in our call, in order to do what God says, and other times we are asked to take a step down in it. David knew how to wait for God's timing (for external accreditation, as it were), but in the mean time, the years were not wasted. Those were the years the warriors of Israel were shaped and guided by his spiritual leadership, so that when the time finally came for a crowning, the undergirding of its military leaders was already in place. It was the same in Joseph's life.

Let's all aim to keep in step with God and not run ahead of His timing and purposes as we exercise our God-given callings.

How to Know We're Dead!

My children used to play the game 'Sleeping Lions'. Pretending to be sleeping so you appeared dead on the floor – the winner would be able to withstand all distractions without waking up.

Likewise, God will allow the enemy to tempt us, but He does so only to test our hearts so that we (God and us) may know if sin is still living in our hearts, so that we can do something about it.

> *Search me, O God, and* ***know my heart;***
> ***Try me,*** *and* ***know my*** *anxieties;*
> *And* ***see*** *if there is any wicked way in me,*
> *And* ***lead me*** *in the way everlasting.*
> (Psalm 139:23-24 NKJV)

The enemy will tempt, but God will test to see if our repentance or our 'death' is complete. As we allow God to sift us, our ability to choose life-giving ways opens up. All the time we are hanging on to our 'old lives' and ways of operating, we will not experience the fullness and freedom God has for us.

Binding the Strong Man

Jesus talks about the authority that needs exercising to subdue the enemy. Using our spiritual gifts to discern the 'strong man' (the enemy in us) in a given situation is really important.

> *But if I cast out demons by the Spirit of God, surely the kingdom of God has come upon you. Or how can one enter a strong man's house and plunder his goods, unless he first binds the strong man? And then he will plunder his house.* (Matthew 12:28-29 NKJV)

Recently, Jasper and I noticed a lot of strange accidents happening around us: car accidents (including a tram going into the back of Jasper's car); accidents happening directly in front of us on the road (that were strangely like the one I had years ago); people hurting themselves at our church and Jasper falling down the stairs. It was happening especially around our church and where we live. Ambulances came up and down our road many times a day, though none for us, thankfully.

I talked to a friend called Trevor, who has a real gifting in praying over regions. He says, you just ask the Holy Spirit to give a name, just like when you are doing prayer ministry and God guides then. As he said those words, it's like the Holy Spirit had known I was seeking and just placed a name in my mind immediately. I didn't tell anyone about it, but decided to act on it as soon as possible.

I know that prayer over regions is best done from a high place so I drove home from Trevor's via the highest place in our area. I bound and cast out the name that had come to mind. That was it. Then, it being late, I went to bed.

The next morning I looked up the word that had come to mind, Kali, and realised it was the Hindu Goddess of death. The name literally means 'lord of death' (we have two undertakers and a crematorium on the road where we live!); since I have prayed and cast Kali out of our region, we have had hardly any accidents in our church; the weird accidents around us and on our road have much reduced and we have gained a new confidence as a church as we prayer-walk with a Spirit-led strategy. I am by no means an expert in the area, but I wanted to illustrate the authority we have over the enemy in areas, not just in our lives.

Our Words as Spirit and Life

> *The words that I speak to you are spirit, and they are life.*
> (John 6:63 NKJV)

Jesus never wasted words – they were all important and worthwhile. Can we all say the same? There are lots of verses in the Bible which encourage us to watch our words. Perhaps one of the most important is:

> *Death and life are in the power of the tongue, and those who love it will eat its fruit.* (Proverbs 18:21 NKJV)

In other words, our words create, just like God's words that said *'Let there be light'*, and there was light.

We should take great care with what comes out of our mouths, knowing that the authority of what we say carries a weight. The following story illustrates the power of the tongue:

I visited Lee Saville's organisation in Romania, called 'Networks', for a few days with some friends. I was deeply impressed with the Spirit-led wisdom and work that is going on there, but was aware as soon as I stepped onto the soil, that there was a great oppression in the air.

One day, two friends and I went for a walk, and a dog kept trying to follow us, running into the road and looking for some attention. One of my friends said:

'Get out of the road, dog! You're going to get run over!'

Being acutely aware of the spiritual oppression I could sense, I slapped him on the back in a half serious, half joking way.

'Be careful what you say,' I said.

Within about 20 seconds, a van appeared, seemingly out of nowhere, and ran the dog over! I was stunned! My friends and I were immediately humbled by the fact that our words really do carry so much weight!

Having grown up in a family of animal lovers, I went over to see if there was anything I could do. I was about 5 feet away and decided to just put out a hand from a distance to pray. Somehow the dog, yowling in pain, leapt to a great height and took hold of my thumb with its jaw and chewed for a moment on it. As I lifted my hand in the air and shook the dog off, I said something like *'oh dear'* (I may have used a few other choice words!) and then, as blood starting pouring from my hand, I suddenly realised where I was. Thankfully, Lee had a doctor in his team who advised a trip to the hospital and a series of rabies injections. I earned the nickname Teen Wolf from a friend because of the experience, but it was rather silly of me to get so close in such a situation.

Our words *do* carry an authority, especially the more 'seated in heavenly places' we become. So use that responsibility and authority to bless whenever you can.

Letting God Do His Job

There will always be people we love and serve who do not respond to us as we would wish, and we are not to be discouraged or preoccupied with them.

Jesus encourages us to 'shake the dust from our feet' where people are not yet open to the Good News we bring. However, most Christians I know misunderstand what I believe Jesus intended: we are to shake the dust from our feet so that we *do not carry anything with us that is negative to where we are going next.* We're not to leave in a *humph*, as if the issue is a personal one! Don't let discouragement, rejection, or frustration come knocking because someone we care for is not yet open and ready. Remember, it is God's job to lead people into truth, it is our job to follow His lead. So pray for them, pray for yourself, and do not be worried or frustrated at all. Remember, we are not to operate in either bitterness or fear!

Where we have relationships that have broken down, and we have done all we can to restore them, but they remain broken, leave it with God to affect them in His time. Sometimes wonderful things come in the end. Sometimes they don't, but it's not our responsibility and we need to be careful we don't *make* it ours.

We Rule Over the Enemy: *He* Doesn't Rule Over Us

> *Look, I have given you authority over all the power of the enemy, and you can walk among snakes and scorpions and crush them. Nothing will injure you.* (Luke 10:19 NKJV)

We are given authority over the enemy by Jesus, to speak to a sickness or the enemy and command them to go. He doesn't plead with the Father, or beg them to go, because His mission and authority are clear. Neither should we!

We are not to plead with the Father to come and heal who we pray for, but we're to command the disease or enemy to '*go*', like Jesus did. I can tell if someone knows their authority by how they pray for illness. I used to think it offensive to talk to the illness. Now I think it is offensive to see the disease as being owned by the person, when really it is just like a parasite.

I pray the same in my personal intercession as I do when I'm praying with people. Where I instead plead with God on behalf of others, it is about spiritual matters, like revelation, healing from brokenness or discovering the truth.

Unforgiveness can be a reason why we cannot shift the enemy when he has taken up residence. We need to stay in a place of forgiveness with ourselves and others, because our authority will be undermined otherwise. King Saul is a sober example of this, and a reminder for us to keep short accounts!

Enforce Your Boundaries

I often hear Christians saying *'I know my legal rights, I know that the enemy shouldn't be stealing from me in this area,'* but they don't really know their legal rights. If they did, they would be enforcing them. I may know that I shouldn't park on a double yellow line, but it's not until I have a ticket that I may refrain from doing so! The law is enforced, but up until that point, I might try and get away with it! Well, the enemy does the same.

Our authority in Christ is not just to bind the enemy. I'll repeat that because it's absolutely key: we are not just called to bind the enemy; we're called to cast him out, to crush his head, to tread on serpents and scorpions.

A lady I know with a son said to me once that her son used to manifest and say some awful things to her. She then described how she would just quietly pray in tongues and bind the spirit that was surfacing and it would immediately quieten. I said to her, *'if you know your authority enough to bind it, then why don't you just go that extra step and cast the stuff out instead of just saying 'shut up and get out of my face!'?!'* So instead I encouraged her to say *'shut up and get out.'*

We all have the authority to cast out the enemy if we're living in the intimacy of son-ship, so go ahead, exercise your God-given right to enforce boundaries.

Where *is* Our Power?

Jesus said that we're to heal the sick (we have power over illness), we're to raise the dead (He's given us power over death), and we're to cast out demons (we have power over demonic activity).

We are to exercise our authority by sending demons packing, but we need to know how to do it. In our society today, even *talking* about demons is distasteful; it's something that raises fear in people, either the language or the concept. Some think of it as archaic and reminiscent of the many injustices which have taken place over the centuries. It's easier to believe in God, or angels, but not fallen angels, and I find that quite ironic.

When we know our authority, we need have no fear. We should not fear the enemy, but because of our history of powerlessness over the enemy in our own lives or others', we can get into fear that things won't change. Let's remember that our histories do not dictate our future:

> *... For as you were once disobedient to God, yet have now obtained mercy...*
> (Romans 11:29-30 NKJV)

> *But now in Christ Jesus* ***you who once were far off have been brought near*** *by the blood of Christ.*
> (Ephesians 2:13 NKJV)

> *For you were* ***once darkness, but now you are light*** *in the Lord. Walk as children of light.*
> (Ephesians 5:8 NKJV)

Our authority is affected by the sin in our lives: if you're having an affair, and at the same time praying for God to bless someone else's marriage, then God isn't likely to honour your prayer. You will know the Lord's favour and blessing in all those areas you have surrendered to him.

> *Confess your sins to each other and pray for each other so that you may be healed.* ***The earnest prayer of a righteous person has great power and produces wonderful results.*** (James 5:16 NLT)

So when praying for others, you need to bring everything under the cleansing work of the cross, to keep your heart and motives pure. We need help to overcome such sins; we need forgiveness from God, and we need Him to show us what to do.

We need to throw ourselves onto God. If we allow sin to be hidden in our lives, then the Lord will expose our sin. It's a bit like in the X-Men films, when Magneto arranged for his prison guard to be injected with metal so that he could be manipulated. It's the same with sin; when we've got sin hidden in our heart, the enemy can manipulate us in that area to do his business.

No Boundary Pushing

When it comes to boundaries, I say to the enemy *'I know my rights.'* I say it quite often in prayers, and when I'm praying for other people, I say *'we know our rights.'* I use Jesus' name, and I'm not just using it like a sticking plaster, hoping that God will bless it, but I'm recognising that what I'm praying for is in line with what Jesus Himself would pray for. I'm praying in Jesus' name, but I'm making sure that I'm praying for what Jesus would want. When I am dealing with the enemy, I don't plead with God to come and deal with the enemy. Where we plead with God to deal with the enemy, we don't know our authority.

Enforce your rights and occupy the territory that rightfully belongs to you:

> *Every place that the sole of your foot will tread upon I have given you, as I said to Moses.* (Joshua 1:3 NKJV)

> *And Jesus came and spoke to them, saying, "All authority has been given to Me in heaven and on earth. Go therefore and make disciples of all the nations, baptizing them in the name of the Father and of the Son and of the Holy Spirit, teaching them to observe all things that I have commanded you; and lo, I am with you always, even to the end of the age."* (Matthew 28:18-20 NKJV)

Knowing Your Rights

CHAPTER 11

Going For Gold

Some of the books in the Bible end with a 'finally, brothers ...' conclusion, which outlines some key things that sum up what the book is about. Here is my '***finally*** ...' collection of thoughts that I hope would be a blessing.

> **Finally, my brethren,** *be strong in the Lord and in the power of His might. Put on the whole armour of God, that you may be able to stand against the wiles of the devil. For we do not wrestle against flesh and blood, but against principalities, against powers, against the rulers of the darkness of this age, against spiritual hosts of wickedness in the heavenly places. Therefore take up the whole armour of God, that you may be able to withstand in the evil day, and having done all, to stand.*
>
> *Stand therefore, having girded your waist with truth, having put on the breastplate of righteousness, and having shod your feet with the preparation of the gospel of peace; above all, taking the shield of faith with which you will be able to quench all the fiery darts of the wicked one. And take the helmet of salvation, and the sword of the Spirit, which is the word of God; praying always with all prayer and supplication in the Spirit, being watchful to this end with all perseverance and supplication for all the saints – and for me, that utterance may be given to me, that I may open my mouth boldly to make known the mystery of the gospel, for which I am an ambassador in chains; that in it I may speak boldly, as I ought to speak.* (Ephesians 6:10-18 NKJV)

Endure for the Prize

> *Therefore we also, since we are surrounded by so great a cloud of witnesses, let us lay aside every weight, and the sin which so easily ensnares us, and let us run with endurance the race that is set before us, looking unto Jesus, the author and finisher of our faith, who* ***for the joy that was set before Him endured the cross****, despising the shame, and has sat down at the right hand of the throne of God.* (Hebrews 12:1-2 NKJV)

My kids were very much open to bribes when they were little – and it worked! E.g. Do this, and you can have a treat! For the joy that is put before us, most of us can endure a certain amount of discomfort. Obviously, Jesus blows that analogy into another realm altogether. But there will be huge benefits for hanging on in there: 'long suffering' does have its rewards.

> *When I'm having a tough time I try and focus on the prize – what I'm aiming for. I'd encourage you to do the same. He conquers who endures.* (Persius)

> *The race is not always to the swift, but to those who keep on running.* (Author unknown, in reference to Ecclesiastes 9:11)

> *"I returned, and saw under the sun, that the race is not to the swift, nor the battle to the strong, neither yet bread to the wise, nor yet riches to men of understanding, nor yet favour to men of skill; but time and chance happeneth to them all."*
> (Ecclesiastes 9:11)

Die Well

One of the most important things we can learn in the Christian life is to die and stay dead (to our old life!). Keep on dying and keep dying well in whatever area the Holy Spirit shows you that you need to surrender to God. As we learn to surrender to God's moulding, the Holy Spirit takes a special delight in us because we're delighting in ridding ourselves of those things which cause Him grief.

Dying should not cause us grief if we are not carrying shame nor condemnation – if we are, then it needs exposing. Just like I have a very different vocabulary now to what I had when I first became a Christian (I could swear the wallpaper off the wall). Likewise, my interpretations of thoughts are radically different, as I discern from a more loved and secure heart.

Guard Your Affections

The enemy can confuse and distract us through our desires when we have yet to develop the character to handle ourselves. I shared about my roller-coaster feelings with regards to Jasper when we were courting. Another example can be an enthusiasm to want to do things I feel led to, but yet not be accountable to my spiritual authority in carrying these things out.

Disorder can come because we want to do the wrong things. Or it can come because we want to do the right things but in the wrong way. If I have impatience, rebellion and control, then I will not want to be accountable to authority unless authority just rubber-stamps my idea. The fruits of the Spirit are attributes that we need in order to live the Christian life in the right way. Patience, kindness, etc.

If we want to save ourselves a lot of grief, then it is best not to set our affection on anything without God revealing we can do so. That way, we guard ourselves from running ahead or disappointment.

Let the Joy of the Lord and His love Be Your Strength

The enemy loves to steal our joy. He really, really does. You already knew that anyway, didn't you, because you have seen the pattern of you getting good news, only for it to be overshadowed with challenges?

There are times when we have little choice over what comes our way. They are the times when we really need our mountain-top times with God. Cherishing our spirit has to be a priority – spending time strengthening our spirit in the Lord.

However, there are times when we have more control over our environment and emotions than we realise. We can choose to see life as difficult, and therefore spend all our strength and focus dodging the problems that come our way. Or we can look at each difficulty with the eyes of faith and opportunity. Rather than difficulties, we have 'challenges'. Rather than problems, we have 'opportunities'. It all depends on how you view them.

> *Now may the God of hope fill you with all joy and peace in believing, that you may abound in hope by the power of the Holy Spirit.* (Romans 15:13 NKJV)

Like I said earlier in the book, *'I can't wait to see how you're going to sort this out'*, there is a quiet assurance in my heart that there isn't anything that will happen that God and I can't sort together. More than that, for every time the enemy means it for bad, there is the seed, the potential for the situation to be a catalyst for a greater good. So, when someone who's been walking with God suddenly turns to drugs, rather than have a mad panic which I would have done a few years ago, I view it as an opportunity for God to do even greater things and I start to rejoice. Yes, that's right. My deep-down pastoral response is to rejoice when the heat gets turned up (obviously not rejoicing at their suffering, but that God is BIGGER than their suffering). I want my confidence in Him to remain steadfast, no matter what is going on around me. We can only do these things with the eyes of faith.

> *Rejoice always, pray without ceasing, in everything give thanks; for this is the will of God in Christ Jesus for you.* (1 Thessalonians 5:16-18 NKJV)

> *For His anger is but for a moment, His favour is for life; Weeping may endure for a night, But joy comes in the morning.* (Psalm 30:5 NKJV)

> *My brethren, count it all joy when you fall into various trials, knowing that the testing of your faith produces patience. But let patience have its perfect work, that you may be perfect and complete, lacking nothing.* (James 1:2-4 NKJV)

Take a Reality Check – Out!

There used to be a phrase that was told in the Church that *'some people are so heavenly minded they're no earthly good'*. I even remember quoting it myself as a young Christian because I felt some people were old-fashioned in their approach to things.

In reality, we can be too *earthly* minded that we're no earthly good. Without our focus on heavenly things, how can we pray these things to earth like we do in the Lord's prayer?

> *Your kingdom come, **your will be done on earth as it is in heaven**.* (Matthew 6:10 NKJV)

Living in the spiritual world is what we are called to. Who wants to invest their time in something which is temporary? I'm all for investing in things which go beyond this life.

Take risks. Live by faith. Get out of the boat! We're to spur one another on to learn and grow in Christ. They say faith is spelt R-I-S-K. Breakthrough is outside your comfort zone, or else you would have it already!

Having Done All, Stand

There may be times when you want to give up, especially when you feel battered and bruised by the spiritual storms of life. Stand.

Let go of the people and situations where your labour of love was not seen or appreciated and leave it at God's feet as an offering of worship to Him. No good deed is ever unnoticed. No kind word is wasted.

> *"And He will set the sheep on His right hand, but the goats on the left. Then the King will say to those on His right hand, 'Come, you blessed of My Father, inherit the kingdom prepared for you from the foundation of the world: for I was hungry and you gave Me food; I was thirsty and you gave Me drink; I was a stranger and you took Me in; I was naked and you clothed Me; I was sick and you visited Me; I was in prison and you came to Me.'*
>
> *"Then the righteous will answer Him, saying, 'Lord, when did we see You hungry and feed You, or thirsty and give You drink? When did we see You a stranger and take You in, or naked and clothe You? Or when did we see You sick, or in prison, and come to You?' And the King will answer and say to them, 'Assuredly,*

I say to you, ***inasmuch as you did it to one of the least of these My brethren, you did it to Me."*** (Matthew 25:33-40 NKJV)

We need never feel used or upset by people viewing us as a doormat, for when we serve God's purposes, we are also doing it for Him.

Work to Your Favour

We will all, as children of God, have special favour in an area. For some, we attract money (!), others get opportunities that are unusual; others have insights that are rare; others always seem to be given stuff, etc. etc.

Don't envy what others have, work with your own favour. It's like an area of blessing that's part of your calling that will bless your ministry. Instead of getting jealous of another's gift, be happy for them and focus on using yours well.

I have a favour to see things. When I ask God why, I find that He tells me. That's mine. What is yours? Do you have a way with people? Do you get given responsibility often? Your favour will suit your calling. Be glad in it and be happy that others have different favours, because that way, we all get blessed in different way.

I find that, as we have this right heart/attitude, our favour grows and spreads to other things. That's motivation enough to press on!

Say What You Mean

But above all, my brethren, do not swear, either by heaven or by earth or with any other oath. But let your "Yes" be "Yes," and your "No," "No," lest you fall into judgment. (James 5:12 NKJV)

To lie or exaggerate is to bring condemnation on ourselves.

> *...put off, concerning your former conduct, the old man which grows corrupt according to the deceitful lusts, and be renewed in the spirit of your mind, and that you put on the new man which was created according to God, in true righteousness and holiness.* (Ephesians 4:22-24 NLT)

Do not grieve the Spirit

> *Therefore, putting away lying, "Let each one of you speak truth with his neighbour," for we are members of one another.* (Ephesians 4:22-25 NKJV)

Every word we speak should be life-giving, hope-filled and true. Anything else is not serving the Kingdom. We are to speak words of encouragement to each other and if we need to speak words that are heavy, they need always to be in love.

Form Partnerships

David had Jonathan. Mary had Elizabeth. Jesus had His disciples. Jesus also had John. Paul had Barnabus. Saul had Samuel. I could go on.

Spiritual alliances or partnerships are all about keeping us strengthened and able to Take Back What The Enemy Has Stolen.

> *Two people are better off than one, for they can help each other succeed. If one person falls, the other can reach out and help. But someone who falls alone is in real trouble.* (Ecclesiastes 4:9-10 NKJV)

Even more than small partnerships, God loves it when we collaborate on a bigger scale, particularly when we're seeking Kingdom goals. Remember that, next time you are tempted to do something solo.

Making God Smile

I believe that, when we overcome, we make God smile. He is happy for us and delighted that we are at One with Him. Here are some of the rewards for those of us who overcome – hopefully they will make you smile!

> *For this is the love of God, that we keep His commandments. And* ***His commandments are not burdensome.*** *For* ***whatever is born of God overcomes the world.*** *And this is the victory that has overcome the world – our faith.* ***Who is he who overcomes the world, but he who believes that Jesus is the Son of God?*** (1 John :3-5 NKJV)

> *He who has an ear, let him hear what the Spirit says to the churches.* ***To him who overcomes I will give to eat from the tree of life****, which is in the midst of the Paradise of God.* (Revelation 2:7 NKJV)

> *He who has an ear, let him hear what the Spirit says to the churches.* ***He who overcomes shall not be hurt by the second death.*** (Revelation 2:11 NKJV)

> *He who has an ear, let him hear what the Spirit says to the churches. To him who* ***overcomes I will give some of the hidden manna to eat. And I will give him a white stone, and on the stone a new name written which no one knows except him who receives it.*** (Revelation 2:17 NKJV)

> ***And he who overcomes, and keeps My works until the end, to him I will give power over the nations.*** (Revelation 2:26 NKJV)

> ***He who overcomes shall be clothed in white garments, and I will not blot out his name from the Book of Life; but I will confess his name before My Father and before His angels.*** (Revelation 3:5 NKJV)

> ***He who overcomes, I will make him a pillar in the temple of My God, and he shall go out no more. I will write on him the name of My God and the name of the city of My God, the New Jerusalem, which comes down out of heaven from My God. And I will write on him My new name.*** (Revelation 3:12 NKJV)
>
> ***To him who overcomes I will grant to sit with Me on My throne,*** *as I also overcame and sat down with My Father on His throne.* (Revelation 3:21 NKJV)
>
> ***He who overcomes shall inherit all things, and I will be his God and he shall be My son.*** (Revelation 21:7 NKJV)

I commit myself to pray for overcomers, that they may Take Back What The Enemy Has Stolen and take hold fully of Who They Are In Christ. Will you choose to be an overcomer? May God bless your endeavours!

Going for Gold

More Information

For more information about the above or LoveF1rst Ministry:
LoveF1rst
c/o The Beacon Church of St Paul's and St Leonard's
331 Arbourthorne Road
Sheffield
South Yorkshire
S2 5HG

Other publications by Tina Hodges
Hurt Without Hate: The Transforming Power of Forgiveness
Soul Care: A Guide To Loving Yourself
Drawing The Line: Protecting What Matters Most

Bogie Busting

Jeff Haynie

Jeff Haynie is a fantasy and illustration artist who has enjoyed expressing his experiences of the world through art from an early age. During his college experience, Haynie gave his life to Jesus, and his artistic work has since evolved into some of the most inspiring that I've ever seen. I would highly recommend visiting his website www.jeffhaynie.com, and particularly his 'Faith Gallery', which includes the cover of this book. I am privileged to have such an accomplished artist feature as part of my book, and I am very grateful for his generosity.

"My faith in Christ has been the very center of my life. Over the years I have painted images that represent major milestones in my spiritual journey. My hope is that these images encourage you to press on toward the high calling of following Christ." – Jeff Haynie.

Laura Jane Craig

Laura Jane Craig is an inspiration. She has built up her own business through hard work, and her God-given gifts, to become an accomplished graphic designer. She has been able to pursue the career she is passionate about, whilst still being able to raise a family. Her designs are beautiful, and she loves to "colour for a living." Her fun sense of humour and unique style make her designs ornate and special. I feel blessed to work with her, and highly recommend visiting her website www.chickenscratchstudio.com